WEAVING A WEB OF MAGIC
A Pot-Pourri of Rituals, Chants, Dances, Webs, Cords, Runes, Talismans, and Magical Information

RHIANNON RYALL

GW00580048

WEAVING A WEB OF MAGIC

©1996 Rhiannon Ryall

ISBN 1 898307 92 X

Cover design & illustration by Daryth Bastin

Published by:

Capall Bann Publishing
Freshfields
Chieveley
Berks
RG20 8TF

Tel/Fax 01635 248711

Dedication

This book is dedicated with heartfelt thanks and gratitude, to all those Pagans of whatever Path, both here and overseas, who gave me their love and support *and* sent lots of positive vibes, during the difficult times I went through.

This included all the people here in Australia, who flooded all sections of the Media with protest letters and phone calls. Two things emerged from this championing of my cause in three Countries; one was that for sheer *"boots and all"* love and support you cannot best a Pagan, and the second very disturbing note that emerged was that *"witch bashing"* by the Establishment is still very much alive and well (we *are* living in the closing years of the *twentieth* century aren't we?).

I shall never forget all the loving, beautiful cards and letters sent me by so many people, many of whom I had never met. Now, when it appears I *may* be vindicated, I will see it as a triumph for all Pagans everywhere, and it should be a shining example to all those others, that just *maybe* we are on the right track. But I shall *never* forget this episode in my life, not least because of the absolute tide of positive thoughts and love that came to support me, from all those wonderful Seekers of the Truth. Truly and from the bottom of my heart, Blessed you Be.

Contents

Introduction

"THE WAY" can be found in the half-realm between sleeping and waking, the twilight lands twixt night and day".

This quotation from a modern-day Celt echoes exactly the concept of the Celts living with one foot in the Otherworld, and working in the times that are neither day or night, neither on land or sea, and so forth. Many of the meditations and rituals in this book are ideally done at those *"in-between"* times and places.

Early twilight on a sea shore with the tide running and an estuary close by, that kind of environment. I cannot describe exactly the contents of this book, as it has so many different strands of magic that are in some instances quite unrelated to each other. They are all pieces that have not been included in my previous books, the reasons for which are varied. Some did not go in because they did not seem to fit into the general theme as I saw it at the time, and some I regrettably forgot about until it was too late! Others were omitted because I have been taken to task somewhat by Pagans from my own era and background who were and still are in some cases, dubious about certain information being published in books.

So this time, I have written to the dissenters and told them of what would be included that could cause them to castigate me yet again! I have discovered that I cannot win; many book reviewers and writers of books on the Craft and allied topics say I do not know what I am talking about, while those in Britain and elsewhere who *know* at firsthand the validity of my writings are constantly plagued with doubts about the knowledge being so freely available! I am still of the opinion that it is better for people to learn old valid stuff and try it out, than wasting time and effort with something that *may* be worthless or at best not have much in it at all. One final comment on how I work and the way I was taught;

Paddy Slade, the British witch/writer, in correspondence with a mutual friend of us both, had this to say, and I quote Paddy's words here as they were relayed to me:

> *"the trouble with groups who do not like Rhiannon's books is that they are not witches - they are Wiccans. Of course her experiences are different. She and I were "born" witches, they have learned "it" from books and don't think of it as a "craft", that is a "hands on" actual "waking" everyday thing. Like Henry V said, "we are but warriors for the working day". Rhiannon and I are witches for the working day".*

So here is a book of a variety of Rituals, Meditations, Magical Information, all manner of magical threads that I hope will lead into a worthwhile Web of Magic for you the reader!

The Glass Tower Ritual

This Rite is similar in many ways to a Ritual of the Druids, and again emphasises there was a cross-over at some time between these two Paths. This Rite is for gaining advice or information, help or comfort. When meditating or working on the Inner Planes, or visiting the Otherworld, whatever name you personally give to this kind of work, I have had much contact with an Archetype who has always been identified to me as *"The Myrddin"*. This is of course the Archetype that is known now as the Merlin in the Arthurian Myth Cycle.

The Glass or Crystal Tower is on top of Glastonbury Tor; in fact it is where the tower stands in this our physical world. It is a round tower this Crystal one, and has a round pointed top. It glints in sunshine. To reach it one must see oneself at the foot of the tor. The tor is composed of grassy terraces, and for the purpose of this Rite, one must climb each one in turn going deosil around the mound, and when back at beginning, going up to the next level.

There are seven terraces in all. When on the last one, you should see in front of you the door of the Glass Tower. These are double doors, Gothic in shape and each has a round bronze handle which turns to open the door. Inside the floor is of flagstones, and in front of you is a winding stone staircase. This goes up in a spiral, and there are thirteen steps and three and a half turns of the spiral to reach the top. The spiral winds widdershins. At the top is a polished wooden door. You knock and enter. If you carry out this Ritual in a Circle, you may physically walk the terraces going around the Circle seven times deosil.

In which case, there is a little poem you can chant as you walk around the Circle, so here is the poem or rhyme to recite:

> *O Wanderer who doth tread the Way,*
> *O Seeker of the Glistening Tower,*
> *that stands twixt starry night and day*
> *in Misty Realms of Truth and Power;*
> *Within the Crystal Turret gleaming,*
> *all thy hopes perceived and weighed;*
> *the silver strands of all thy dreaming,*
> *unravelled and before him laid.*
> *Thy Destiny he will foresee*
> *if thou true courage steadfast show;*
> *then Guardian he will surely be,*
> *protecting ye where ere ye go;*
> *with Mistle, Yew and Apple Tree.*

Apple and Yew are correspondences for the Crystal Tower. If working this in the Circle, or even just by yourself, you may care for a drink other than the normal Circle wine. If you have the following, drink it *before* you do the Ritual, although of course you could still have some afterwards if you make enough.

Here is the drink:

Get some roasted Hazel nuts, grate them and boil them up in spring or rain water.

Add honey and a pinch of cinnamon.

This is usually drunk when hot, but it would not matter if it had cooled down. You need a good quantity of nuts however, and need to really stew them to get the flavour into the drink.

If you are uncertain how to reach the Tower, or have difficulty generally with *"getting"* anywhere in these kinds of workings, I have included here a couple of ways that seem to work quite well.

The first one is to visualise a sloping woodland on the side of a hill, which is slanting away from you. You walk down and in the trees, there is an old fashioned door standing upright. On the door, you can see the words written *"Glass Tower"*, or a picture of it, whatever suits you best. Then open the door and go through and you will be at the base of Glastonbury Tor. Or you can count down twenty one steps, starting at twenty one and finishing at one, then going through an archway and seeing the Tor, or you can float through rainbow coloured clouds and on landing be at the base of the Tor.

Most of this kind of work is easier in a Circle, even if working alone, as the atmosphere is already there to assist one. But if doing Inner Planes type of working indoors, then of course using meditation breathing is a good idea.

Traditional Month Names

In my book *"Celtic Lore & Druidic Ritual"*, I mentioned the old Devonshire names for the months and also the dates of them. In Somerset they had slightly different ones, and the Devon list had quite an attractive rhyming mnemonic to assist the memory. As an item of interest, I thought I would include them in this book and for those who are unfamiliar with my other writings, I will repeat the Devonshire list here too.

13 Moons or Months

Date	Devon	Somerset
Nov.12 - Dec.9	Hunting Moon	Weaving Moon
Dec.10 - Jan.6	Knife Moon	Spindle Moon
Jan.7 - Feb.3	Plough Moon	Seed Moon
Feb.4 - Mar.3	Primrose Moon	Water Moon
Mar.4 - Mar.31	Axe Moon	Withy Moon
Apr.1-Apr.28	Scythe Moon	Peat Moon
Apr.29 - May 26	Milk Bucket Moon	Fleece Moon
May 27 - June 23	Stream Moon	Flower Moon
June 24 - July 21	Blackberry Moon	High Summer Moon
Jul.22 - Aug.18	Grain Moon	Barley Moon
Aug.29 - Sept.15	Sickle Moon	Garnering Moon
Sept.16 - Oct.13	Cider Barrel Moon	Apple Moon
Oct.14 - Nov.11	Snail Shell Moon	Mummers or Dodman Moon

I will explain some of these titles later on, but first I will give the little rhyming mnemonic for remembering the Devonshire names. I do not know if Somerset people also had this little device, but to date I have not come across it if they did, so here is the Devon one over the page.

Dog Fox barks upon the hill
the Hunter in the Vale below
sheaths his blade and turns to go
where the fields new-ploughed show
by hedge-row rimmed pale blossoms blow.
Beside the byre stacks of wood
of last Summer now is stood
cut in billets for the fires
that the handy scythe-man burns
while his mate fills full the churns.
By the stream small children merry
gather baskets of Blackberry
take them past the barn where stored
is last Harvests golden hoard.
Bill-Hook hanging on the wall
above the cider barrels tall
and outside on wet, green grass
see old Hod-Me-Dod slowly pass.

It will be noted that there are marked differences in the life-style of these two Counties, looking at the Month names. Some of these must be incredibly old, as for a very long time now, the two economies have been almost identical. However if one goes back far enough, the Somerset people relied very heavily on basket making. They also burnt peat on their fires, but at the present time I have no idea where in Somerset the peat bogs were. Perhaps a reader could enlighten me.

Apples of course have always been an important crop in both counties and also highly significant from a magical point of view. The most significant would have been the final month which included Samhain, and this is reflected in its symbology.

The *"Hod-Me-Dod"* which is a Devon word for snail, (I remember as a child, my Grandmother called the individual bunches of hair that were tied up in *"rags"* to produce ringlets, *"Hod-Me- Dods"*, because they resemble a snail, with the knotted piece of rag and the two ends resembling horns), snails come out in wet weather, but more importantly their shell has a spiral on it, which can represent death and re-birth among its many correspondences.

In Somerset they had the *"Dodman"*, that strange figure who walked boundaries and ley lines with two staves in his hands. The staves presumably reminded people of the snails horns, and maybe that is why he had that particular name. He was also linked with death and therefore re-birth, as the ley lines he walked, normally led to old barrow mounds - the ancient grave sites of our ancestors.

There does seem to have been, in the West Country at least, a mystique regarding snails, it is possible the main reason for this is the spiral design of their shells. All the words of the months quoted were originally in Anglo-Saxon, and as spellings change often meanings do also. It is hard sometimes to decipher what was originally meant by a particular word, especially when its modern counterpart has a completely different connotation to the original.

The prime example of change is the word *"wicce"*, that is for another day! However the word *"wistful"* in Anglo-Saxon meant having plenty of food a full larder in fact. As a matter of interest, the Anglo-Saxon lexicon used *"H"* as the first or final letter, as in *"Hwoete"="wheat"*, and all the modern words that commence *"sh"* and are derived from Anglo-Saxon were in their original form spelled with *"sc"*. In common with the early Gaelic, (that of the *"Q"* Celts), Anglo-Saxon had no letter *"P"*. It had a *"th"* pronounced in the usual way, and it is interesting to note that it had a symbol which is the same as the Nordic Rune *"Thurisaz"*.

In Anglo-Saxon dictionaries today, the words that would start with the letter *"P"*, still have printed in them the Rune that means *"thorn"*.

To return to explaining the old West Country month names; *"knife"* month which was sometimes called *"killing"* month, because of hunting, but more so because they had to reduce their herd numbers owing to lack of winter feed. *"Plough"* Moon is obvious as is *"Primrose"; "Axe"* month was for the laying in of fuel ready for the following winter, *"milk-bucket"* is for the flush of milk that comes with plenty of grass, next month the streams are quite full, the next two are self evident being *"blackberry"* and *"grain"*, then *"sickle"* for clearing unkempt Summer growth particularly in hedgerows, cider barrel for apple cider of course, and then *"snail shell"*, which I have already discussed.

Webs, Cords, & Hag Stones

Web magic is so old that it probably goes back to the very earliest times. It could well be one of the first magics ever worked with, as the people of that time would have utilised spiders webs. There is something magical and awe inspiring about a spiders web, it is so delicate and perfect, that no doubt to primitive folk it would have seemed to be magical in its own right.

Cords, webs and nets, appear in the mythology of so many races, and do seem to fascinate most people at some time or another. Occultists among others are aware that everything is connected by a silver web, which crosses time and dimensions, so that we can be or are connected to the Otherworld in addition to *all* on this Plane of Being.

So to do cord magic, it is a good idea and enhances the work to incorporate the silver web. The web can also be used for the purpose of meditation and may make easier the getting to where ever one wants to be, by vitalising a strand of web which one can use as a guide rope as it were, to reach ones objective. So if several people are working cord magic, first visualise an old blackened oak tree stump, and from this stump is flowing a strand of silver thread. Then incorporate this thread into your cords as you weave them and see a web of silver being formed.

You use this web and cords on the physical plane of course, to contain an illness and tie it up tight and remove it, or you can put a wish into each knot, or remove negative vibes from a place or house.

You visualise the web with its burden being cast into deep water with a stone on it, or buried under a stone, and you do this on the physical with your cords. You do this even if it is for a wish, except the intent of course is entirely different.

The reason for the water or burying, and the reason for the oak tree, is because this kind of magical working is attributed to the Elder Gods, that tradition has it, live under the water and therefore also underground. I think this idea of them being under the sea, is a garbled tale that has come down to us because of the submerging of Atlantis, but after all these years the concept has a validity of its own and therefore works. Years ago people used fishing nets for this kind of Rite, partly maybe because that connected directly with the sea. I don't think the colour of the cords is important, except to the person doing the magic, so any colour you feel is appropriate should work well.

Using A Hag Stone

This is used when for some reason you need a temporary boost of protection around your house. That is the most common reason for using one.

You need a stone or pebble that has a hole right through it. This *must* be a natural hole, not a man-made one. I have picked up three such stones over the years on the beach. They do not need to be large, but they must have the hole created by nature - not by a human hand! Take the stone into your Circle or working area, pass it through all elements, then with the same water draw a symbol on the stone that identifies you. Then you call on a Goddess energy, such as Medb or even the Morrigan if you feel the situation warrants it, and visualise her essence going into the stone. You could even use the Crone aspect of the Goddess. You explain the reason you need her and also draw a sign that identifies her. Then you put the stone on your gatepost. When the need is over, take the stone back into your Circle, thank her and quite firmly tell her she is released and may go. Then wash the stone in Circle water, and if you have used a very fierce energy, it is wisest to throw the stone into the sea or deep water or to bury it.

If you bury it and mark the spot, then after a year and a day, it should be alright to retrieve it to use again. I realise that to discard the stone forever seems a waste of all the trouble you may have had finding one, but it is better when using the darker aspects to give them no excuse for hanging about! I did this Ritual on one occasion, and on the day the unwelcome caller was due, I had a visit from a very sweet gentle lady who was a *"New Ager"*, and one I call of the *"White Light"* brigade. She almost fell through my front door, looking very uneasy indeed and asked me if I had *"done anything"* over my front gate. I said I had, and she told me that she had to make herself come through the gate as all she felt like doing was running away. The unwanted caller did not turn up after all, so whether it would have worked so well on a much stronger personality I never found out. To trace the symbols and to remove them, use a Willow wand *not* a knife.

Another modern use for a Hag stone could be if you were going somewhere at a time of day and in an area where you could be nervous, then you could put one in your pocket or handbag. In this day and age it could be a good idea!

The Enneagram

When used in a dance for raising energies three women and six men normally dance the design. The energies are gathered up at point nine and then channelled out between points four and five, into the land. It was normally danced before the first day of Spring and was to assist with re-vitalising the earth energies before Spring planting. The design is drawn on the ground to reach the perimeter of the Circle, and is drawn with one of the usual materials, i.e. salt, chalk, quartz chips or mustard seed.

There is no particular music or song for this dance, but it should be neither too fast or too slow. Something like the *"Skye Boat Song"* is a good tempo.

To commence, the three women each stand on three, six and nine, the six men on the other points.

They all move deosil when stepping round.

They all trace the pattern three times, then the woman at point nine moves forward slightly to gather the energies, as the others go in this way:

4, 3, 2 and 1, move to 9 touching each point as they go and now they move in either direction - deosil or widdershins.

So 1 goes to 9,
8, goes to 9,
2 and 7 go to 1 and 8 respectively, then on to 9, 3 and 6

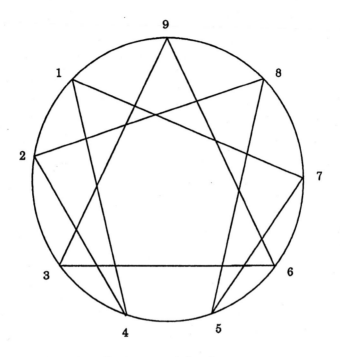

go to 7, 2, 8 and 1 respectively, then on to 9.
4 and 5 go in the same manner.

At Nine they all stay near the woman at 9, but leaving
her slightly in front.

They then assist her to spread the flow of energies down
through the gap between four and five, out of the Circle
and see it spreading out and moving over as much land
as they can see, and visualising it moving on past
physical sight.

When this is finished there should be no energy left in the
Circle, as the Enneagram drawn to the Circles perimeter will
have used it all, through dispersing it. The Enneagram glyph
drawn without the feminine triangle, is the Druid symbol for

"Oak". The masculine numbers of this design are very peculiar. Taken in the order in which they are drawn they are:

1,4,2,8,5,7, (then back to 1 again)

These numbers if multiplied by any of the numbers two to six inclusive, simply move along the line. I will show some here to demonstrate:

142857x2=285714
142857x3=428571
142857x4=571428
142857x5=714285
142857x6=857142

If multiplied by seven, the answer is all nines. If one wished to multiply by fifteen for example, one method would be as follows: 142857, then move them thus:

714285, but place them under the first figure so that the 7 is under the 4 of the first number, add them together and you have 2142855, which is the same as multiplying the original by 15.

The sequence 142857 is of course related to *"pi"*. If this number for *"pi"* is shown in decimals, you have 3.1428571.

If any number consisting of 1 and a random number of zeros is divided by seven, the smallest set of numbers produced as the answer is 142857, the next one is 1428571, then 14285714 and so on. One can see how the ancients regarded numbers with awe and saw in mathematics a great mystery of the Universe, as indeed did Pythagorus.

The Flowers of the Mineral Kingdom

Crystals are a miracle of nature. It is not surprising that so many people are fascinated by them. Their vitalising force can assist us both physically and spiritually. When first purchasing a crystal, it should be placed in an earthenware bowl that has been filled with rainwater or spring water. Into this water a small handful of rock or sea salt should be dissolved.

The crystal is then placed in this water for at least twelve hours. If possible it should be placed in a sunny position for part of that time. This will cleanse the crystal of any stray *"negative vibes"* it may have absorbed passing through so many uncaring hands before it reached you. When you have *"bathed"* the crystal dry it carefully, and do not let anyone else touch it. The water must be disposed of down the sink. Do not throw it on the garden.

The clear crystals are masculine, the opaque are feminine. Smokey quartz is a powerful crystal. It should only be used for healing when the person has very low vitality. Very depressed, or feeling low after illness, that kind of situation can be alleviated with smokey quartz. A single piece of it should be placed point towards the soles of the feet, while healing with other crystals is carried out.

Amethyst quartz is a great purifier and healer. It assists greatly with the healing of skin disorders, painful eye conditions and nervous disorders. Of course, the main purpose in the use of crystals is for spiritual cleansing and soothing. Also for enlarging our knowledge and awareness of the Unseen World. The etheric body through utilising the Psychic Centres or Chakras, may be cleansed by the use of crystals.

The crystal is held point towards the Psychic Centre, commencing with the Crown. You visualise light streaming in from the crystal, and at the same time rotate the crystal deosil. Rose quartz is good for the heart Centre. When you have completed a healing place your crystals in the sunlight to revitalise them. Only use single crystals for cleansing Psychic Centres, as clusters and large crystals may send out too much energy. Amethyst assists to raise our level of consciousness and can be useful for people who have low opinions of their abilities.

For general healing of a person, they can be laid down and clear crystals placed pointing at the soles of the feet. A clear crystal and one of Amethyst can be pointed down to the top of the head. Rose quartz or opaque plain quartz are angled to point at the palms of the hands, and the ears. The energies are then seen flowing through and clearing. A large clear crystal can be used to sweep the Aura.

Hold the crystal in the right hand and with the point facing the person, sweep deosil right around the body. Start and finish at the crown of the head. Do this sweeping fairly slowly and you may find it needs more than one sweep. Afterwards use a Rose quartz and see all positive and peaceful energies flowing in. When attempting absent healing, it is a good idea to try and "see" the person surrounded by crystals. They can be seen as producing a white or blue light.

In addition, you may see the person enclosed by a blue pyramid, from which flows energy. The pyramid has an upright crystal in the apex and out of this, flows any sickness or negatively and is dissolved in the ether.

Crystals can also be personalised for your own use. Take it in your hand immediately after it has been cleansed, and holding it level with your eyes point towards you, emphasise mentally and very strongly what you wish the crystal to be for. Remembering important dreams for example. In this case you would keep it under your pillow, point towards the bed head. In the morning hold the point in the region of your third eye and try not to force the issue, but relax through meditation breathing. Never use a clear crystal though, as they are too active. Use an opaque female one. Never leave crystals in your bedroom with the points towards each other. At best it will stop you sleeping, at worst it will give you a rather bad headache.

If you wish to wear a crystal as a pendant, make sure it is a double terminated one. This ensures a two way flow of energy for you. You can also use this as a pendulum. Crystals can also be used for meditation. A cluster of Amethyst is good for this - try it in your Circle, you may be quite pleasantly surprised at the result.

Crystals come under the dominion of the Moon, so if using them for healing, phases of the Moon may influence the result. Crystals are also linked with the Constellation of the Pleiades, so although they seem to be a bit of a 'new-agey' type thing, they were in use in Atlantis, and are a very valid artifact for us.

There are many uses for crystals; I know of some people who fasten them on their carburettor as they say they get more miles to the gallon. Others fasten an Amethyst close to their skin in the heart or solar plexus area to aid them mentally in their every day life.

Crystals are one of the "building blocks" of our Planet. All is essentially based on a crystalline structure. The Qabalistic diagram known as the Tree of Life, is based on a crystal.

There are those who attempt to find past lives from crystals, as they are like the memory bank of a computer. What is not always realised though, is that crystals from a particular location, will only have memory of that area-it will only pertain to the part of the world where it was growing.

There is a theory that if one could obtain a crystal from the stones at Stonehenge, then learn to unlock it, all the past uses of Stonehenge would be revealed. Crystals remain one of the most enigmatic and powerful natural artifacts we have.

The crushed pieces of crystal that are sometimes available from where we have regrettably plundered our Planet, can be placed on the soil where we grow our plants, and they will then improve, be more pest free and grow more vigorously. This use of crushed crystal remnants is one of the methods of natural husbandry espoused by the late Rudolph Steiner.

Using Crystals In The Circle:

A crystal can be placed in each of the four quarters, two male and two female. Place them so that candle light shines through them. They can be stood in little glass containers, that have sea or rock salt in them to keep the crystals upright. This can be done for the Glass Tower Rite, or one can be held.

If the crystals are placed in the quarters at the New Moon, they can be linked with a ring of salt, then salt is placed in a ring around the fire. From the quarters a straight line to the ring of salt around the fireplace. This is for Invoking the Goddess Arianrhod, as her Castle was a silver wheel.

Some Colour Correspondences

Red: Strength and Vigour

Orange: Kindness,Adaptability, Stimulation, Encouragement, Plenty.

Yellow: Confidence, Joy, Charm,Comfort.

Green: Energy, Growth, Fertility, Charity.

Blue: Tranquillity, Understanding, Patience, Devotion, Sincerity.

Indigo: Dignity, Impulse, Ambition.

Violet: Sentimentality, Power.

Colours and the Signs of the Zodiac

Aries: Red
Taurus: Yellow
Gemini: Violet
Cancer: Green
Leo: Orange
Virgo: Turquoise
Libra: Gold
Scorpio: Sea green
Sagittarius: Purple
Capricorn: Blue
Aquarius: Magenta
Pisces: Indigo

Celtic Meditations or Inner Planes Journeys

These are based on the Tree Ogham, but I have included other correspondences in order that the reader has a choice of symbol to work with. Some find one glyph easier than another to use when attempting this kind of work. The other correspondences are Herb, Colour and Bird Oghams. There are thirteen of these journeys for the thirteen consonants, which is all the Celts used, and of course, five vowels. The vowel ones are slightly different, as vowels were always so important and mysterious. (See the Hebrew Alphabet).

According to the Druids, the nine lettered name of the Goddess was all vowels. Interestingly enough, they claim there should be thirty two Paths on the Hebrew Tree of Life (which it would appear is older than the Hebrew Race), the reason for the number of Paths being that it took thirty two strokes of the original Ogham to carve this nine lettered name. This was when the Oghams were either straight or slanting strokes cut into a line along a piece of wood, before it became more complicated and diverse - a very long time ago indeed!

All the little *"Journeys"* here are quite short, but of course when one gets used to this form of working, they will expand if one chooses to learn more.

Working With *"Beth"*

Tree: Birch

Colour: White feathers

Herb: Mullein

Bird: Pheasant

You are in a forest on a Spring morning.

The trees are Silver Birch and the leaves have only just opened.

A pathway winds through the trees, but its destination is not visible.

Walk along the path and follow its twists and turns.

The woods are very peaceful. Every now and again, you will see white Doves fly from one tree to another.

You *may* meet an old Shaman who will be squatting down on the ground, wearing a white feather cloak.

Go over and speak to him.

Working With *"Luis"*

Tree: Rowan   Herb: Rue

Colour: Floodwater grey   Bird: Duck

You are in a small wooden boat, on flat grey water, that has no ripples in it. While you sit there, wondering how you will reach the shore as there are no oars in the boat, you see a great cluster of Rowan trees covered in berries, all along the Eastern shore.

Then you realise that the water is not large after all, only a small pond and shallow.

Step out and go over to the trees.

Look at the leaves and berries. You will get an intuitive *"flash"* that is very meaningful to you, and you will suddenly fill with energy and positive happy vitality.

Working With *"Nion"*

Tree: Ash

Herb: Herb robert

Colour: Clear as the wind

Bird: Snipe

You are on a high hill, green, but with no trees. It is very windy and as you look around you, a light mist comes, blocking out any sight of the horizon.

You walk towards the mist. As you move forward, the mist clears and in front of you is a small village with a Blacksmiths Forge.

You can hear the Blacksmith at work.

Go over to the forge and speak to the Blacksmith.

You may find that he is crippled, so be prepared for that.

Working With *"Fearn"*

Tree: Alder

Colour: Crimson

Herb: Celandine

Bird: Gull

You are walking along the side of a stream. It has a grassy bank, but at the bottom of the slope towards the water, the flat base of the bank is very fine little stones. These can also be seen through the clear water of the stream.

An old woman is standing by the side of the stream, she has grey hair in a bun, a long black skirt, a white apron, and a red shawl around her shoulders, which is held in place by a round, silver brooch.

On a tripod she has a big black iron pot, boiling over an open fire. In the pot is cloth she is dying red, with the sap from a stand of Alder trees that are nearby.

She will speak to you if you go over to her.

Working With *"Saille"*

Tree: Willow

Herb: Mugwort

Colour: Grass-green

Bird: Hawk

You are beside a broad, flowing river whose banks are lined with Willow trees, all with young leaves on their branches.

A young woman, with long blonde hair, and dressed in a long flowing gown of light green, is walking under the trees. She is playing a flute type of instrument.

As she plays the notes, they float out in the air like little teardrop shapes of golden light, then they drift away.

Look into these golden drops before they are gone and you may see little pictures in them.

In any event, stop the young woman and speak to her.

Working With *"Huathe"*

Tree: Hawthorn

Herb: Chamomile

Colour: Silver/black

Bird: Crow

You are at the entrance to a great, glowing cave. It is not dark inside, or cold, but warm and full of light.

You enter.

The walls appear to have polished gem stones in them.

The floor is covered with soft green moss, that does not feel damp.

Walk through the cave and you will come to another exit. It leads out on to a smooth green lawn, surrounded by a hedge of Hawthorn bushes. These are not trimmed, but are growing in a natural unkempt manner.

A woman dressed in white is sitting by one of the bushes.

The woman's arms are full of Hawthorn blossoms and she is looking into a small mirror.

Walk behind her and you will see that she is not looking at her reflection, as the mirror shows scenes of life.

Speak to her, and she will show you symbolic views for your help and guidance, in the mirror.

Working With *"Duir"*

Tree: Oak   Herb: Rosemary

Colour: Charcoal grey   Bird: Wren

You are in an Oak grove. Within the grove is a circle of granite stones. A firepit is in the middle of the circle, within the stones. It is full of black charcoal.

A shaft of sunlight is slanting through the trees, and strikes the firepit with a golden light.

A small pool of water is in the West, but inside the stone circle.

Walk over to the pool and gaze into it as if it were a crystal ball.

There may not be anyone in the circle, but you *may* meet a grey robed figure, who will at first appear to be an old man, but on closer inspection is actually a youth.

Working With *"Tinne"*

Tree: Holly

Herb: Comfrey

Colour: Iron grey

Bird: Starling

It is a winters day.

You are walking in a garden.

Along the right hand side, are several Holly bushes covered in red berries.

An old couple, both with grey hair, walk up to the Holly bushes. The old woman is carrying a set of scales made of pewter. The old man gathers berries and they weigh them in the scales.

Go over and speak to them.

Working With *"Coll"*

Tree: Hazel   Herb: Nutmeg

Colour: Brown   Bird: Crane

You are standing in front of a ploughed field. Around the edge is a strip of grassland about nine feet wide. At the far end of the field is a small copse of Hazel trees.

Walk along the grassy strip until you come to the trees, and underneath them on the ground is a woven basket. It is full of Hazel nuts.

Pick out nine nuts and cast them on the ground as if they were Runes.

You will either see patterns on the shells that advise and guide you, or the pattern they make as they fall will answer you.

Working With *"Muin"*

Tree: Vines   Herb:Yarrow

Colour: Brown/black   Bird: Titmouse

You see before you an archway covered in Vines. The floor is laid with square tiles of black and white.

The Vines have branches laden with grapes, but they are both black and green varieties.

At the end of the tiled path and archway, is a bridge over a little stream. On the other side of the bridge, is a similar archway covered in Vines.

Walking across the bridge is a man and a woman. One is leading a black horse and one is leading a brown horse. Between them rides a child on a piebald pony.

Speak to them.

Working With *"Gort"*

Tree: Ivy

Herb: Sage

Colour: Blue smoke

Bird: Mute swan

You are looking at an old castle. There is not much left of it, except one tower. The ruin and the tower are both covered in Ivy. It is not gloomy however, as the day is sunny, and the Ivy is the variegated kind.

Go inside the tower and you will find a man and a woman who are studying together.

The room is filled with blue smoke, but it is not the sort of smoke to cause coughing, it is misty and smells like some kind of incense.

The two peoples robes are the colour of the smoke.

Go up to them and they will talk to you.

Working With *"Ngetal"*

Tree: Reeds or Dwarf elder   Herb: Vervain

Colour: Sea green   Bird: Goose

You are on a sea shore. A turtle comes up from the sea, lays her eggs, covers them and returns to the water.

The sea is green rather than blue, with lots of white foam, but it is not stormy.

As you stand looking at the turtle returning to the water, along the beach comes a sort of chariot. It is drawn by real horses, not sea horses and the man standing up in the chariot, looks like a warrior-king.

He is bearded, about forty five years old. He is wearing a robe fastened by a brooch made of three rings joined together. His hair is held back by a gold circlet, which has three points on it.

The man is full of vitality. He will drive his chariot into the sea and under the waves.

Speak to him before he disappears.

Working With *"Ruis"*

Tree: Elder   Herb: Heather

Colour: Blood red   Bird: Kestrel

You are standing by a group of Elder trees. Under the trees, nine people are dancing in a circle. There are five women and four men.

An old man is sitting under one of the trees playing some pipes for them to dance to. He is dressed in a dark red robe, patterned with white Elder flowers.

When the dancing finishes, you notice that all the people have the same robes on.

All ten of them then stand around the edge of the dancing area, as if they are going to commence a Ritual, or start another dance.

Go up to them before they start again.

If you have a question, ask it.

Working With *"Ailim"*

Tree: Silver fir

Herb: Plantain

Colour: Black/white (Piebald)

Bird: Owl

You see yourself in a Temple.

The walls are hung with silk in bands of black and silvery white. These are vertical bands, so that the walls are striped, but in very broad bands.

In front of you is a stone Altar. On this is a silk cloth of the same two colours, and in the middle of the Altar is a black stone bowl, from which violet smoke is rising. A seven branched candlestick of silver is on the Altar to the left of the bowl. In it are seven lighted candles which are violet in colour.

Wait at the Altar.

Working With *"Idac"*

Tree: Yew   Herb: Nettle

Colour: Shiny white (like snow)   Bird: Rook

You are standing in a snow-covered landscape. There are no footprints in the snow anywhere. On the left is a stand of Yew trees.

Go over to them and you will see standing in their shelter, a woman and a small boy, who are waiting to take you to a little cottage close by for shelter.

When you are all sitting by the open fire in the cottage, the woman will *"read"* the fire for you, scrying with it as if it were a crystal ball.

Working With *"Ur"*

Tree: Bell heather   Herb: Red clover

Colour: Honey or amber   Bird: Raven

You are standing in a smallish field on a lovely Summers day. There are many flowers in the grass and you can hear the hum or drone of Bees.

In front of you but a little way off, is a row of bee-hives. A man is tending the hives.

Go over to him and he will take out of one of the hives, a whole honeycomb. Within the hexagons of pattern, you will see or know in your mind an answer to a question which is vexing you.

If this does not happen, ask the man for an answer to your puzzle.

Working With *"Onn"*

Tree: Gorse OR Furze   Herb: Thyme

Colour: Dun (as a newly ploughed field)   Bird: Plover

You are standing on open ground, with Gorse growing quite freely. Over to the right, is an Oak tree which has Mistletoe growing on it.

There are three figures by the tree, one is in Blue, one in Green and the third one is in Red.

The Mistletoe is green with white berries on it.

However, the three men are cutting a piece of Mistletoe, and this particular branch is golden.

Go over and speak to them.

The one in blue is young, under twenty five, the one in green is about forty and the one in red is an old man.

Working With *"Eddha"*

Tree: White poplar   Herb: Fennel

Colour: Rufus red   Bird: Curlew

You are walking along a lane lined on each side with White Poplar trees.

You see a gate to an Apple orchard, open it and go into the orchard. The apple trees are laden with full blossom, but at the same time, they are also heavy with ripe apples.

Some mice are under the trees, eating windfalls.

Stand and watch them. You will see that as they nibble away the apple, the seeds fall out and the mice scrabble with their paws to cover the seeds with earth.

The seeds immediately begin to send up little shoots.

Sit under a tree and either empty your mind, or think of what you have seen.

Someone will come and talk to you about the reason you chose this particular Working or Meditation.

The Forgotten Meanings in Children's Stories and Other Writings

Most people know that the rhyme *"Ring-a-Roses"* refers to the plague; also that *Humpty Dumpty* was the ill-fated Richard the 3rd. But some tales are an almost forgotten and garbled account of Rituals. Mostly of Rituals of Initiation. Kisses exchanged for example, are concerned with the Initiator breathing Higher Consciousness into an Initiate, so releasing them from only being aware of the physical, earthly world. *"Sleeping Beauty"* is a prime example, and the Prince hacking his way through a tangle of brambles, is the removing of ignorance, and emphasis on worldly matters. Being asleep, is a common enough phrase of implying that someone is unaware, Ouspensky saw the citizens of a city walking past him with their eyes closed. He realised this was not an actual fact, but that was how they appeared to him in their unawareness.

The Minotaur and the Labyrinth are obvious memories of Initiatory Rites. The Minotaur being the lowest, basic, physical side of human nature. Many Initiates in the Mediterranean area at that time used a labyrinth in Initiations. Ariadne was the Higher Self leading Theseus through the maze towards higher consciousness, when his more animal side was left behind.

Any Hero from that era and location whose name ended in *"eus"*, was on a Quest of some kind.

The most glaring example of Rites jumbled, half forgotten and then turned into a children's story, is of course,"Snow White". It has so many elements of a Ritual, (even though like the Arthurian Cycle, good has become bad), that one hardly knows where to begin. The glass coffin that Snow White was laid in is the Glass Tower used for Initiation. The Queen, (Crone?), can shape-shift, or again, the emphasis *had* to be on witches being *"bad"*. The Seven Dwarves are probably seven psychic centres or chakras, which would include correspondences with the seven Planets. The Queen had a *"Magic Mirror"*, used as a form of scrying, apples abound in old myths and this one would *not* have been a poisoned apple. It is the *interpretation* because it would have had Pagan magical connotations, the apple was therefore, *"poisoned"*.

The piece of apple lodging in Snow White's throat is a very interesting concept, as it is connected with speech, maybe she could not relay her knowledge because without a full Initiation, she did not fully comprehend it. The Prince *"kissing"* her, breathes the life of an aware psychic into being and then she can speak. Maybe the not speaking is a euphemistic way of alluding to oracular pronouncements, and her ability/inability to give these.

I was taught that any story that has a glass or crystal artifact in it would most likely be a tale based on a jumbled and distorted version of Ritual. This does not apply to *"Cinderella"*, where the slipper was not in fact made of glass in the original, but fur.

A mistake in translation from the original French, has given us a slipper made of glass, which should be of fur.

"Beauty and the Beast" is obviously allegorical, and so maybe are all those frogs that turn into Princes. I have been working for some considerable time on the old song *"Green Grow the Rushes O"*, as I believe the words are in many instances most

likely incorrect through distortion and language changes. Many of our words were originally Anglo-Saxon. Their alphabet had no "P", no letter "V", (the same as Gaelic in this instance), and some words that now begin with "Y" originally started with "G" or "E".

Meanings change also. With reference to *"Green Grow the Rushes O"*, line three says *"three three the Rivals"*, which most people find a bit of a puzzle, as rivals are normally only two people; also what are they rivals about? Well, in the original Anglo-Saxon, the word was spelt *"Ryval"*, and meant a man who earned his living by fishing from a river bank. He was known as a *"ryval"*, so if another man was also fishing, but from the opposite bank, they would both have been *"ryvals"*. So that presumably is how we now use the word to mean two people in opposition with each other, a quite different meaning from the original.

"Nine for the nine Bright Shiners", are the nine names of Odhinn, or nine Anglo-Saxon gods, as all the Norse god names come as I have said previously, from a very old root word meaning *"shining"*.

In line six I do not think it was *"Proud Walkers"*, but I do believe the second word to be a distortion of Anglo-Saxon *"wealcan"* meaning *"to roll"*, and was applied to the Sun quite often. Six being concerned with the Sun, (or three sixes anyway), I think this is what it would be.

If any reader has knowledge of the old meaning to this song, I would very much like to hear from them. I have done a little more work, but I just wanted to demonstrate here how easily errors creep in and how difficult it can be to correct them, or even identify what they should be, when so much time has passed.

To return to nursery tales for a moment; *"threes"* are prolific in early childhood stories:

3 wishes,
3 little pigs
3 blind mice,
3 bags of wool
3 bears

the list is almost without end.

"Winken, Blinken and Nod", are three godforms. Woden or Odhinn, Baldur and Nodens. (Sometimes the *"alter ego"* of Nuada). *"Blinken"* is from the Anglo-Saxon *"Blicen"*, which meant *"glitter"*, so we are back to the *"Shining Ones"* again, a title which certainly suits *"Bright Baldur"*.

It is interesting to remember that in the nursery rhyme Winken, Blinken and Nod, *"sailed off on a river of crystal light, into a sea of dew"*. The Celts in particular held dew to be of great significance and used it as an allegorical word in many mysteries, in particular those connected with the Old Gods or Old Ones.

As these Megalithic People worked the Dark Moon Cycle of the Goddess, with all that is implicit in *that*, so the Gods worked with at that time in history (or pre-history), were perceived mainly as the male generative force, the ignitor of life if you like, so *"dew"* had another meaning altogether.

While on the topic of word interpretation and meaning, often the red-eared hounds that Herne leads, were called *"Ratchet Hounds"*, or simply *"Ratchets"*. The general supposition is that the pack are leading departed souls to the Otherworld. *"Ratchet"* is from the French word *"Rochet"*, which means a spool. A ratchet wheel drives old fashioned clocks. It can also be a bar or piece of mechanism turning at one end upon a pivot, while the other end falls into the teeth of a wheel or rack, allowing the latter to move in *one direction only.*

A ratchet wheel, having angular teeth into which a ratchet may drop, stops the wheel from running *back.* So calling the hounds *"Ratchets"*, seems to be appropriate and logical, if they are gathering up the departed.

The emphasis on *"mills"* is another peculiarity of old ways and also in folklore. It would be because people saw sky and earth as a wheel turning, or perhaps two mill stones grinding. Arianrhod's Silver Wheel for example, also called the Revolving Castle. This would be the turning of the heavens. Incidentally, the old Gaelic word for turning anti-clockwise is *"tuathall"*, for those who may wish to use it; after all, Deosil is Gaelic as those who have driven a car in Dublin and read street signs will know!

With regard to *dew ponds;* as a child I viewed them with awe, considering them without being told, as very magical places. Because we are composed of much fluid and because our Planet has so much sea on its surface, I think we all have a great affinity with water and its Elementals. It may be if there are one day, Planets found with intelligent life, they may have a particular element that is appropriate to them, and that ours is water.

A Dew Pond is like a large Cauldron of water and can be used as a Circle, particularly if working with the element of water. That Dew Ponds frequently occur on crossings of Ley Lines, will come as no surprise.

I have encountered *"Horse Whisperers"* in my time, but I have never found anyone who knew how to make a Dew Pond. The water from them is excellent for cleansing crystals, and may also be used in a Circle, or for Consecrations of any kind. On a crossroads of Ley lines, they make the design of the Celtic Cross.

To use them *as* a Circle, you need to make the boundary a few feet around the edge so that you have some ground to work on. It is also a good idea to have crystals in the Quarters in addition to candles. In this instance, fires would be rather misplaced, as water is the prime element.

Working With Both Sun and Moon

(This Rite can be worked by two people or with a full group).

If two people only, then the Rite can at closing, be Tantric. It is carried out when both the Sun and the Moon are visible together in the sky. Either very early dawn or just before dusk, both times of day are suitable.

The herbs to be burnt are those of Sun and Moon. The Fire herbs can be Bay, Chamomile, Juniper, Marigold, Oak or Rue. Water herbs can be Balm, Mallow, Purslane or Willow.

The man or men stand in the South, the woman or women stand in the North. They concentrate on bringing the two energies into the centre of the Circle.

This mixed energy flow can be used to empower Cauldron water, if working Cauldron magic; it can be channelled into a working tool to charge it when consecrating a new one, a Wand for example, or it can be poured into a person for balancing, or poured into the Earth. It can also be used to charge up a Talisman for a particular purpose.

An Ancient Saxon Curse

I include this old form of *"smiting"* an enemy, not because I consider anyone should use it, but it *is* a curiosity from long ago, and in its own way, quite comprehensive!

> *"I curse ye by a Right line,*
> *a Crooked line, a Simple and a Broken.*
> *By flame, by wind, by water, by a mass, (i.e.*
> *a solid lump), by rain, by clay.*
> *By a flying thing, by a creeping thing, by a*
> *serpent, by an eye, by a hand, by a foot,*
> *by a crown, by a cross, by a sword, and by a*
> *scourge, I curse thee.*
> *HAADE, MIKADED, RAKEBEN, RIKA, RITA-LICA,*
> *TASARATH, MODECA, RABERT, TUTH, TUNCH."*

I believe the last eleven words to be a form of counting, similar to that of the ancient Lincolnshire shepherds and also those of Sussex. These were as follows, and were for counting sheep:

1. Yan	2. Tan
3. Thethera	4. Pethera
5. Pimp	6. Sethera
7. Lethera	8. Hovera
9. Covera	10. Dik
11. Yan-a-Dik	12. Tan-a-Dik
13. Tethera-a-Dik	14. Pethera-a-Dik

15. Bumpit	16. Yan-a-Bumpit
17. Tan-a-Bumpit	18. Tethera-Bumpit
19. Pethera-Bumpit	20. Figgit

Those above were the Lincoln ones, below are those for Sussex:

1. One-Erum	2. Two-Erum
3. Cock-Erum	4. Shu-Erum
5. Seth-Erum	6. Shath-Erum
7. Winberry	8. Wagtail
9. Tarrydiddle	10. Don

A couple of things about this Sussex form are interesting; one is that the numbers four and five commence with Egyptian deities names, number four for being female and number five male, also our word *"tarrydiddle"* meaning *"nonsense"*, must have its origins in this old form of counting sheep.

Number ten *"Don"*, is one form of a Celtic godname, so there is quite a mix in these old words of counting.

In *"Celtic Lore & Druidic Ritual"*, I mentioned a set of four symbols that can be used in the Quarters particularly at Lady Day and at Midsummer. There was also a little rhyme to be chanted when drawing these.

I mentioned too, that I had been informed it is known in Orkney Island Craft. There is another use for these symbols, but first for those who may not have read *"Celtic Lore"*, I reproduce the symbols overleaf:

East:

South:

West:

North:

The rhyme that accompanies the tracing of these Sigils is as follows:

In the East the silver streams,
In the South the fire gleams,
In the West the boughs lean down,
In the North the Quarters crown.

Each of these symbols has a tree correspondence. These Sigils can be traced on the human body, and when this is done they untie or release the energies in the body, so that if carried out at a Final Initiation for example, it will generally assist the Initiate to connect with the Otherworld easily, and it also enhances ones intuitive abilities and the Art of *"Seeing"*. This should *never* be done at a First Initiation, for what I would hope, are obvious reasons.

The way these symbols are drawn on the body is as follows:

Overhead the Sigil for the North,

On the chest and stomach the Sigil for the South,

Over the thighs and legs the Sigil for the West,

Then over the whole body from about throat height down, the Sigil for the East.

No words are spoken while this is done, the little rhyme is only for drawing these in the Quarters. In any case, one needs to really concentrate when drawing these on a person. There is in fact a set of verses that starts off with the little rhyme, and then goes on to suggest or hint at the other use for these symbols. Here it is in its complete form:

In the East the silver streams
In the South the fire gleams;
In the West the boughs lean down,
In the North the Quarters crown.

So the folk of Hill and Lea
know this well - it is their Lore;
But those who have the eyes to See
the Inner Wisdom, know the Four-conceal Another-
and the Truth of these Woods
is hidden well;
As the kernel of the nut
nestles there inside the shell.
But the Guisers in the cold
of Mid-Winter know the Truth
that Hazel, Willow, Oak Fruit all

enclose the Silver Streams that fall.
As the Hazel inside its shell,
hides until discovered be;
so the Birch concealed by all
lives and shimmers magically.

As the bonds that bind a slave
can with Inner Strength be loosed;
So these Ancient Symbols show
the Way to open minds to Truth.
The fetters of the everyday
that hold the mind with thoughts deceiving,
are cast aside, and now the Soul
Ancient Wisdoms is perceiving.

The wood associations are:

East	Birch
South	Hazel
West	Willow
North	Oak

This is a very powerful way of opening up to energy, and the symbols are some of the very earliest used by mankind, or at least, the earliest that have been found in ancient stone carvings.

Deciphering and Understanding Celtic Mythology

I feel I have been rather ambitious with the heading of this section most likely, as the Celtic system for want of a better word, is like a tangled ball of wool! Particularly as much of the tangle is intentional. However, as so many of those who have either read my other books or attended my seminars want to have the tangle unravelled, as much as I can I will do so here.

To understand and decipher the Celtic philosophy, one must understand their legends. The biggest stumbling block to sorting the wheat from the chaff, is the regrettable overlay of what one might call the *"Christianisation"* of these myths. There are some writings however, that have not been tampered with in this way, but they themselves are full of cloaked meanings and allegory. There are clues to be found in them nonetheless, although written down after the Christian era commenced.

The text of the *"Lebor Gabala"*- the Irish *"Book of Invasions"* is one such text. It begins with the arrival of Partholon and his people to Ireland after the Flood. There is much merit in the view held by some that the stories of Partholon and Nemed, are of the same events and with the same people. One of the arguments for this is that Partholon begins with a *"P"*, and the *"P"* Celts are later than the *"Q"* Celts, who, as I stated earlier, did not have the letter *"P"* in their language. Some writers say that Nemed was a Greek from Scythia, but as the Celts were known in both these areas, it would be feasible to suppose that Nemed may have come from that area of Europe. There are tales that state when some of these emigrants were driven out by later tribes, they did in fact go to those countries.

At the time when Nemed invaded Ireland, the people then in residence were the Fomorians, (who were reputed to be the off-spring of Chaos and Old Night), an earlier group of the same ancestry as the Nemedians. The word Fomorian simply means *"those who live under the sea"*. This would be very significant if one subscribes to the view that the Atlanteans became submariners after the Deluge, and would give credence to the story of Oannes the *"Fishman"*.

There is a school of thought which postulates the theory that the Atlanteans built underwater cities, and resided in them for many years after the destruction of Atlantis.

The Nemedians and Fomorians fought off and on for many years. Even after the death of Nemed the two groups still struggled for supremacy. Then came the Fir Bolg, who conquered all, and divided Ireland into five Provinces.

What has to be born in mind, is that all these different peoples originated from one race or geographic location. They intermarried, spoke the same language, had the same customs more or less, and their religious rites were opposite sides of the same coin.

Then came the Tuatha de Danaan, they too were of the same rootstock. Legend has it, that their ships sailed through the air and landed in Ireland. All these groups have one myth or incident in common, namely they *all* burned their boats when arriving on the shores of Ireland. The Tuatha de Danaan, were descendants of Nemed and his people, Nemed's Grandson being one of the de Danaan.

It is the Tuatha de Danaan who brought the Magical Weapons with them from the Islands of Finias, Falias, Murias and Gorias, where the de Danaan taught Magic and Ritual. The implication is not clear that they came directly from these islands, and I believe that these four islands, together with the unnamed *"Sacred Isle"*, would have been the last pieces of land that were above water for a time at te submerging of Atlantis. There were three calamities before the whole of Atlantis or all the islands that were known collectively by that name, sank. These five may have been the very last to be submerged.

Whatever the actual course of events, the de Danaan did bring the weapons with them to Ireland. Tradition has it, that all these separate groups of emigrants or invaders, landed on the first of May, of whichever year each group arrived. This would imply some overlay of Ritual connected to each group as May Day is so important to the Celts. It also reinforces the statement that these diverse groups were originally from the same homeland, as they all ad this magical day.

The final invasion was led by Mil and his Milesians. It is generally accepted that the Milesians came from Spain. They were probably te *"Black Celts"* mentioned by Tacitus, and would have been in marked contrast to the de Danaan who were most likely fair haired Celts. Both the Milesians and the de Danaan had a Druid class in their social structure. After Mil invaded, it was the Druids on both sides who battled for supremacy. Incidentally, *"Mil"* was not the leaders name; once again, it simply meant *"Champion"*, so in common with the gods, we do not know his personal name.

It was finally agreed that the two Races should share Ireland. Mil told the de Danaans that they could have the land underground, while he and his Milesians would rule the surface.

It is from this that the idea has come of the *"Fairy Folk"* living in hollow hills. The name of the under hill villages is the *"Sidhe"*, and this has come to mean both the location and the name of the people themselves.

This is, of necessity, a very *"potted"* version of Celtic myth and folklore. Apart from the *"Lebor Gabala"*, the *"Book of Ballymote"* is the only other Irish source of these myths, but very few copies exist outside Ireland.

The Welsh *"Mabinogion"* is of later date than the Irish works. It is an established fact that at one time, the Irish invaded Wales and partly colonised it. The *"Mabinogion"* has to be even more sifted and deciphered than the Irish works.

All Pagan Druidic ritual is based on the premise that it is of Atlantean origin and that the gods have a light side and a dark side, or that two kinds of energies are worked with. The Fomors only worked with the dark or heavy energies, the de Danaan with the light. This may be where the idea arose that the Fomors came from under the sea, as their gods were chthonic. The Milesians worked the same as the de Danaan. The Druids of course, saw polarity and reconciling balance in everything.

One of the difficulties with sorting out the Celtic god forms is that different tribes at different times, had their own names for the gods, and some Heroes also, were give a gods name and over the years all this has become intermingled.

The Megalithic peoples of Britain may have been the same race as the Fomorians, or at least from the same time frame. They worked with the heavy energies in a similar manner to the Fomors, and therefore worked with vortex energy, whereas the de Danaan worked with a cone.

This cone of energy is where the concept of a tall pointed hat has come from. It is shown as being worn by dwarves in addition to wizards and also of course, witches, although it is masculine energy and the vortex is feminine.

In order to clarify all this rather confusing information, I will explain the two forms of *"Otherworld"* symbology used by all these people. But first, I will explain some of the energy sources that both groups of Druids or Shamans worked with.

Their magical technology if one can call it that, involved the use of energy spirals in the ground. These manifest as either clockwise in direction or counter clockwise. The opposite energy to a spiral, is one contained in a straight line. The lines are either positive or negative also, and generally where they intersect, a spiral is formed. Because we live in a three dimensional world, all magical workings are involved with either cone or vortex shapes of energy.

This also applies to the lines and spirals. A vortex and an anti clockwise spiral are feminine, a cone and a clockwise spiral are masculine. A positive Ley line is masculine, a passive or negative one is feminine. In some instances the Roman roads of Britain are on Ley lines.

The energies would be dormant if not dead by now, with the amount of traffic on them. Historians have always been loud in their praise of the beautiful straight roads the Romans built, but they were only utilising that which was already there.

The Romans did not bother to discover there was an esoteric reason for these tracks, in any case, they were not interested in the beliefs of the native population. They had no idea that the tracks so conveniently marked that they built their roads over, were the energy paths or the earth's spiritual veins. These Ley lines cover the whole Planet.

There are two systems; those that run North to South and are magnetic and those that run East to West and are etheric. The Greeks who had knowledge of these lines, considered them to be the embodiment of the Earth's Spirit, and named them *"Magnes"*; whether they were aware of the two different directional flows and considered them both magnetic, or were only aware of the North South flow, I do not know.

Stonehenge was built to link Cosmic, Solar and Earth energies, and by so doing reinforce and regenerate the Planetary energies that sustain the earth, and everything on it and in it. Of course there is not only one reason for Stonehenge, it has been modified by people with different uses in mind over a very long period of time. There are apparently, three distinct stages of the structure, but one of them was to utilise this combination of energies.

Of course there are the Great Tides as well. As I have written of these previously, I will not go into detail of them here, but will simply point out the differences in the two sets of rhythms. The Ley forces ebb and flow, dawn and dusk being the times of day when the energy peaks. The Great Tides have a rhythm that depends on the time of year, and for the Celts their cross-quarter days came inbetween the changes in the Great Tides.

These energies are the vibrations that all occultists of any persuasion, work with whether knowingly or not. The Great Tides while having a Seasonal rhythm, also change at the two Solstices and the two Equinoxes. Ley energy is picked up and amplified by standing stones and this would be one reason for their placement in the landscape.

Needless to say that the Moon is also considered to affect the energies in some ways. The Great Tides for example, change within themselves during the passage of the Moon the polarity can be affected from the New Moon onwards. That most ancient people knew of these things would seem to me quite logical. The Druids for one worked these energies, and so I would imagine did the Norse Shamans.

These Nordic races had so much in common with the Celts, particularly the Druids, that they seem also to have sprung from the same rootstock. The underlying structure of the *"Odhinnic Mysteries"*, and other Norse Rites are so similar that I believe my assumption to be valid. The Norse Mythology has never excited the interest that generally is found in with the Celtic lore, whether Irish or Welsh.

Yet within the framework of the Norse myths and their rather *"Conan the Barbarian"* type of godform, is concealed a complete and detailed system that is very similar to that of the Celts.

The only facet of Norse Ritual which has captured the notice of Pagans generally, is that concerning the Runes. Apart from the few who practice Runelore as an esoteric system, and even then more would be interested in the Runes as Divination, than as a workable, complete system.

In common with most Celtic deities there are nine magical names for Odhinn, or nine god forms with certain characteristics depending on how one views them. If one looks at them as nine facets of one god-form, they are divided into into triads. They can of course be worked with quite easily as nine individual god-forms.

I list here the nine names, the arcane meaning, appropriate colour and the Tree from Tree Ogham which seems to apply.

Name	Colour	Meaning	Tree/Trees
Odhinn	White	Inspiration	Rowan
Vili	Blue	Light Aspect	Ash
Loki/Hadhr	Orange	Dark Aspect	Willow
Baldur	Violet	Young Warrior	Hawthorn/Oak
Hoenir/Mimir	Turquoise	Cognitive/ Reflective	Holly
Ve	Red	Re-Birth	Hazel
Lodhurr	Magenta	Arcane/ Knowledge	Ivy
Bradi	Green	Poetic	Dwarf Elder
Heimdallr	Yellow	Guardian	Elder/Birch

Because the two systems are not identical, and because within one system there are differences due to tribal names, older or later attributes etc., the lists cannot be absolutely clear cut or fit perfectly.

There is a system that divided the above yet again, into nine worlds or Spiritual Centres, very similar to the Celtic Psychic Centres, or the Eastern Chakras.

The Norse Shamans as would be expected, worked with Cone and Vortex. Some of the very early pre-Runic symbology were used as Sigils to enhance or alter the polarity of either cone or vortex. Another very Celtic Druid piece of arcane work. Some of the symbols used in this manner were from the ancient Hallristinger Script, these having the attributes of either active, passive or neutral.

That the Nordic and Germanic races had a system of Priesthood that was of similar philosophy to that of the

Druids even in its methodology, is confirmed by the writings of both Tacitus and Caesar. The triadic view, the sacred groves, that kind of custom are the same for all three.It was this priesthood that used the Runes for Divination. They were similar to the *"glory twigs"*, spoken of in the Anglo-Saxon *"Nine Herbs Charm"*, which were Rune staves carved from small tree branches. Numbers three and nine were of significance also, nine glory twigs being cut but only three used for *"reading"*.

The Circle of the Runemasters was similar to a Druidic Gorsedd, and of course to a Craft Circle. Rune Masters wore red and carried a Staff; so do Druids. Both Shamans or Rune Masters as with the Druids had a Mistletoe Cult, one has only to think of Baldur to see this. The quite obvious similarities are striking. The Norse system is very powerful, but of course it has its dark or heavy energies too. It is well to remember that the Rainbow Bridge not only goes *up* to Asgard, but *down* to the darker realms.

The Fomorians had among their Pantheon one who was called Balor, and Balor possessed only one eye, which tradition says was blue. This was not a cyclopean eye, it was simply that at some time one of his eyes was damaged. In the Irish legends Balor is depicted as being evil, but this is from a de Danaan point of view. To the Fomorians, he was a revered and honoured god form. Balor is of course one of the Dark Gods, symbolising the heavy energies.

Now the accepted picture of Odhinn is a tall figure, wearing a cloak and a hat with a large brim. The hat is pulled down over one eye, or rather the eye socket, as the actual eye is missing. His solitary remaining eye is blue, and Odhinn is accompanied by a Raven and a Wolf, two very *"Dark"* Celtic creatures. Folklore tells us that he often appears at crossroads.

Odhinn is a particularly Shamanistic type of god form. The de Danaan Tradition, which is still alive and well today, although only taught to people of certain blood lines, has a Creation Myth which demonstrates to a certain degree, that they too have a link with the Druids. Briefly this myth states that the Goddess gave birth magically to another aspect of herself, which was masculine. This god in his growing time was seen as of a blue hue, in his youth as green the Green Man - the Foliate God, and in his maturity as of a ruddy or reddish hue. These colours are of course, the three colours of the Druidic Degrees.

As I have said earlier, one of the problems with Celtic lore is the almost fanatical cloak of secrecy within which it dwells. We all know that the Druids disapproved of the written word. Even the Welsh *"Triads"*, very difficult to obtain, are not clear in their meanings. One has to know exactly *what* is being referred to, for a comprehensive grasp of the subject matter.

A good example of an allegorical tale which has several layers of meaning, is that known as the *"Spoils of Annwn"*. Taliesin is the Bard who recites these verses, but whether he is the author remains unclear. The events referred to in this poem, take place in the Celtic Otherworld, in the Under-World in fact, and at *one level* are most likely a voyage on the *"Inner Planes"*, although in certain lines there is an inference of an Initiatory Ritual as well. The lines that refer to Arthur, *may be* a later addition to the poem, but probably before it was ever committed to the written word.

I will give the poem in its entirety, and then will attempt some explanation of its various meanings, although I am by no means an expert on the verses.

"The Spoils Of Annwn"

I will praise the Sovereign, supreme Lord of the land,
Who hath extended his dominion over the shore of the world.
Stout was the prison of Gweir, in Caer Sidi,
Through the spite of Pwyll and Pryderi;
No one before him went into it.
The heavy blue chain firmly held the youth,
And before the spoils of Annwn woefully he sang,
And thenceforth till doom he shall remain a bard.
Thrice enough to fill Prydwen we went into it;
Except seven, none returned from Caer Sidi.

Am I not a candidate for fame, to be heard in song
In Caer Pedryvan, four times revolving?
The first word from the cauldron, when was it spoken?
By the breath of nine maidens it was gently warmed.
Is it not the cauldron of the chief of Annwn?
What is its fashion?
A rim of pearls is round its edge.
It will not cook the food of a coward or one forsworn.
A sword flashing bright will be raised to him,
And left in the hand of Lleminawg.
And before the door of the gate of Uffern the lamp was
burning.
When we went with Arthur-splendid labour!
Except seven, none returned from Caer Vedwyd.

Am I not a candidate for fame, to be heard in song
In Caer Pedryvan, in the Isle of the Strong Door,
Where twilight and pitchy darkness meet together
And bright wine is the drink of the host?

Thrice enough to fill Prydwen we went on the sea.
Except seven, none returned from Caer Rigor.

I will not allow much praise to the leaders of literature.
Beyond Caer Wydyr they saw not the prowess of Arthur;
Three-score hundreds stood on the walls;
It was hard to converse with their watchman.
Thrice enough to fill Prydwen we went with Arthur;
Except seven, none returned from Caer Golud.

I will not allow much praise to the spiritless.
They know not on what day, or who caused it,
Or in what hour of the serene day Cwy was born,
Or who caused that he should not go to Goronwy in the dales
                                                    of Devwy.
They know not the brindled ox with the broad head-band,
Whose yoke is seven-score hand breadths.
When we went with Arthur, of mournful memory,
Except seven, none returned from Caer Vandwy.

I will not allow much praise to those of drooping courage.
They know not on what day the chief arose,
Nor in what hour of the serene day the owner was born,
Nor what animal they keep, with its head of silver.
When we went with Arthur, of anxious striving,
Except seven, none returned from Caer Ochren.

The name of Arthur.s ship; *"Prydwen"* means *"Fair Face"*, according to the experts, although I would have thought it meant *"White Face"*, wen meaning white. However, it *may* apply to the god Ogma, whose name means *"Sun Face"* or *"Fair Face"*.

Ogma was the god who invented Ogham, and it is said that he was the same godform as Apollo and Hercules, both of them having attributes of the Lion and the Sun. It is also said that

Ogma, who was of gigantic proportions, carried a club, wore a lion skin, and drew crowds of prisoners in his wake, who had golden chains attached to their ears, the other ends of the chains being attached to the tip of Ogma's tongue.

These *"prisoners"* were obviously the letters of the Ogham, Ogma speaking them and the *"prisoners"* hearing them, or even that the prisoners were in fact the letters themselves. It is a very clear allegory of the Ogham alphabet. What this has to do with *"Arthur's ship"* I am not sure. Line three tells of Gweir who is also Gwydion, being held on an island by a *"heavy blue chain"*. This chain is of course the sea surrounding the island.

Caer Sidi is the Spiral Castle, Caer Pedryvan the four cornered or revolving Castle. This may apply to the Planet Earth as it revolves around the sun, or it may be the four seasons that are cyclic. Caer Vedwyd is the Castle of revelry, Caer Rigor the kingly Castle; Caer Wydyr is the Glass Castle and Caer Golud, or as it is called in some versions Caer Colur, is the gloomy Castle. Caer Vandwy is the high Castle and Caer Ochren is the Castle of the sloping sides, or shelving sides.

These eight Caers or Castles refer to the Celtic Psychic Centres of the body. They are not in the order in which they appear on the human frame, but are in the order to place eight Festivals around the Axe of Light. They are also part of Castle Ogham.

The 'seven only' that returned would, I believe, be the seven original Planets known in ancient times, as the Caers can be applied to the constellations in the sky. Line twenty in the second verse which refers to the lamp burning before the gates of Uffern, probably refers to the Moon. The lamp being the Moon, as *"Uffern"* means the *"cold place"*.

Lines fourteen to eighteen in the second verse, refer to the Sacred Enclosure, the pearls about its edge being Druids standing around the perimeter, (this is quite a common blind) and the line stating it will not cook for cowards or those forsworn, means that only the brave and true Initiate can be allowed to receive higher knowledge, the way into the Gorsedd being guarded by a Druid with a sword.

The brindled ox with the broad head-band referred to in verse four, is the Zodiacal Taurus. It states that his yoke is seven score handbreadths, in some translations it states he has seven knobs on the collar. These are the seven stars of the Pleiades, which are in the constellation of Taurus. It may be these seven stars not the old Planets that are referred to.

The Milky Way was known as the *"Castle of Gwydion"*, so it would seem likely there are references here to the skies in addition to the Underworld.

The Island of the Strong Door, confirms that in part the poem relates to Druidic Ritual, as door and oak are synonymous in many instances as indeed are oak and Druid.

There are probably many other meanings to this poem, but are either lost or kept very guarded by today's Druids. Line ten in the penultimate verse which refers to Goronwy in the dales of Devwy, is difficult; *"Goronwy"* means the *"seat of the Moon"*, but I have no idea where the dales of Devwy may be.

One final comment on all of this; when the poem was used as a series of *"keys"* for Inner Planes working, it would have been with vortex energy as the Celtic Underworld is female in polarity. These Dark Cycle workings are extremely ancient going back to the Fomorians and then the Megalithic people of Britain.

There are still those today who work this way, and they are known as *"Wessex Craft"*. They have nothing to do with the new *"Wicca"* movement, and are presumably still largely unknown to the modern Wicca Path followers.

We now come to Godnames, which is a very difficult topic to unravel. According to some experts on Scandinavian Mythology *all* the deities names are based on an extremely ancient rootword which meant *"Shining"*. So all the Norse Pantheon would be collectively *"The Shining Ones"*, and that is what their individual names mean.

It is somewhat similar to Hebrew Mysticism where all the different names for god, simply mean *"Lord"*. I explained at length about this confusion, in *"Celtic Lore & Druidic Ritual"*, with regard to the Arthurian Myth Cycle. *"Mider"*: An Underworld god. Connected with the Isle of Falga, which is the Isle of Man, therefore Mider is also Manannon, who could be viewed as an Underworld god, because his castle is on the sea bed.

Ogma also called Cermait, meaning *"honey-mouthed"* and *"sunny-faced"*, is the god of literature and eloquence. Not surprising in the inventor of the Oghams. His wife is *"Etan"*, daughter of the god Diancecht, who is god of medicine and healing.

Goibniu-weapon-maker, i.e. a Smith god. Lugh his father was one of Diancechts sons, who married Ethnui, daughter of Balor, who was of course a Fomorian god.

The majority of deities mentioned in Irish writings are those associated with the Tuatha-de-Danaan. I will ignore the Welsh names as that makes it even more confusing, and anyway Lugh or Llugh, is also a slightly later deity than the others, arriving when arable farming commenced and then became part of the Irish Pantheon.

Nuada was a war-god and he was killed in battle with the Fomorians. *Bile* was husband to the goddess Danu. The *Dagda* who was the chief god form, had a wife called Boann, which would connect her with the river Boyne, so she may well have been a river goddess. The Dagda's children were, Brigit, Oenghus, Mider, Ogma, Bodb the Red. Oenghus was called *"Oenghus Mac Og"*, meaning *"Young God"*, or *"Son of the Young"*. He had a golden harp.

Brigit was the goddess of the hearth fire and of poetry. The Dagda had a harp made of oak. There were four warlike or warrior goddesses, the chief one was *Morrigan* or *"The morrigan"*, and Morrigan means *"Great Queen"*. The other three were:

> *Fea*-means *"hateful"*
> *Nemon*-means *"venomous"*
> *Badb*-means *"fury"*

The group word for them was *"Badb"*, or supposedly, *"the Furies"*.

Balor the Fomors god, had a son called *"Elathan"* and he was described as a *"beautiful man with golden hair on his shoulders"*; a mantle of gold, five golden necklaces, (torcs?) and a brooch of gold with a shining precious stone. Two silver spears with rivets of bronze and his sword was golden hilted and golden studded. (Obviously Bronze Age not Iron). He had a son called *"Bress"*, which means beautiful.

The old Underworld god Crom Cruach was possibly Fomorian, but the words *"Crom Cruach"* only mean *"Lord of the Mound"*, or *"Bowed One of the Mound"*, so once again we have no idea of his actual name.

When working with the light aspects of deities, the Watchfire (see Celtic Lore & Druidic Ritual), is associated with three

Celtic gods. They are Oenghus, Brigit and Lyr. With the inclusion of Lyr, they would be of later origin but still a very long time ago. Bran who is usually associated with the Watchfire, and who became an oracular head, has a counterpart in Norse Mythology, where Mimir's head was buried by a well, and was also oracular.

Early Peoples and the Zodiac

The Sun, the Number 72, Other Knowledge from the Ancient Mediterranean Peoples

While it can be seen that much knowledge is hidden within old Celtic material, it does not just apply to that particular system, or indeed to Witchcraft in a general way.

The following items have nothing to do with the Craft, but do demonstrate how easily information can be misunderstood and misinterpreted, and also show how some of our knowledge has come from sometimes surprising sources.

Most of us know that the *"SUN"* became confused in the last two Millennia with the *"SON"*. The Sun was originally perceived as a symbol of the god of our Universe - a Solar deity in fact. However from the confusion of a Solar God with the Sun-God, came a whole mathematically based system, which while built onto this error is valid as far as it goes and works.

In the following pages this and other allied matters are dealt with in what I hope is an interesting and informative manner. I repeat they have nothing to do with the Craft per se, but the information is quite enlightening, which is why I have included it in this book.

This does help to clear up a few puzzles concerning ancient peoples, and explains some anomalies in writings, especially those dealing with the Signs of the Zodiac.

Because the Sun became of prime importance, much study was undertaken of its passage across the heavens.

Some of this is still evident in Hermetic teachings. According to the Golden Dawn, there are 72 Quinances, with each having a Guardian Angel. This number 72, featured very prominently in Hebrew lore. The Old Testament is full of *"seventy two's"*. To investigate further into this number, three days are 72 hours, so six days are 144. This is the number of squares marked out on the floor of a Freemasons Temple and their Rule is 24 inches in length. Ceremonial Magicians also have the identical floor layout.

Half the squares are black and half white in both instances. Quite logical because everyone thinks of twelve hours of day light and twelve of dark. In fact this only occurs at the two Equinoxes, which are very important indeed to both these Temple workings.

The arbitrary six days of creation were obviously set as the number already had spiritual connotations. For countless hundreds of years, science and religion were contained together within the Priesthood. Not just the Semitic people, but all priesthoods were aware of geometry, natural ores, other substances that could be used in an esoteric manner, and of course healing.

Much earlier than the rise of the Hebrew Tribes, many cultures were the custodians of arcane knowledge. The Universe is based on mathematics and these ancient Gurus were aware of this and its general significance. When deciphering their arcane mysteries 72's pop up every-where, including multiples of the number and parts thereof. That it is allied to the sun's passage and therefore the Zodiacal emblems are obvious.

The Sun loses about one degree every 72 years, and this could be where the mystique around this number originated. Seventy two conspirators aided Osiris, assassin. Plutarch says that this occurred on the 17th day of the month of Athry, when the Sun was in the constellation of Scorpio. The scorpion (among other things), symbolised treachery. If Osiris was *"slain"* at or near the end of a 72 year cycle, then the 72 conspirators are simply the years that brought that particular Age to its close.

The Bull was sacred to Osiris, so it would be at or near the end of the Taurean Age that this event took place. Now before the reader puts this down in disgust and says I am wrong and this could not be, having previously spoken of Scorpio, let me explain how this occurs, and confirmation may be found in many books written by very learned people.

Apparently there are two systems pertaining to astrology and its application. One of these which dates from the time of Ptolemy, and is called Geocentric, is based on the premise that the Earth is at the centre of our Solar System, and that all the Planets, the Sun and the Moon, revolve around it.

While from an astronomical point of view it is wrong, for thousands of years it worked accurately when applied to the material side of earthly things. That the most important occultists were aware of another system can be observed by a close study of their writings and diagrams. This other system is called *Heliocentric* and places the Sun in its correct position, at the centre of the Solar System, with all the other Planets revolving around it. This must be born in mind when looking at other information available to us. I will return to this topic later, but for the moment I want to look at those enigmatic seventy two's.

In Israel Regardie's book *"The Golden Dawn"*, there is a note which deals with the forming of angelic names. It says that various verses are taken from the book of Exodus, and by methods of permutation are formed into 72 names of three letters each.

To each of these names is added the suffix *"Yah Orel"* thus yielding angelic names and formulae. These 72 angels are allotted to each quinary or division of five degrees in the heavens, so that with other names a very complete hierarchy is given. Ultimately, every sign of the Zodiac has an archangel, angel, angel of its corresponding house, and a massive sub-hierarchy.

This great plethora of angels does seem to me to be a touch superfluous, unless of course, there are corresponding heavier forms to pair them with and create balance. There is no mention of any other form and it does seem very lopsided and lacking in the very balance essential for this kind of work, and *why* this great multitude of angels anyway?

There are two items of interest in this extract; one is the number 72 yet again, the other that it reinforces the view the Old Testament *has* knowledge in it, but it is hidden, and the writings *cannot* be taken literally.

The 72 angels would appear to have their inception in the Atlantean teachings. They perceived five worlds a bit like the five worlds associated with the Qabalah. According to this system-the Atlantean one, each of the five worlds is ruled by an Element. Each world having five sub-planes also ruled by an Element. Twenty five planes of being in all. This set of fives and the twenty fives applies in one way to the islands of Atlantis. The quinances apply to these worlds.

They also apply to the 72 acupuncture points on the human body. There are more than this, but 72 are the main ones. So the passage of the Sun across the Macrocosm, is mirrored in the Microcosm - Mankind - as the little Universe. There are also 72 killing points on the human body, which are taught in some esoteric Martial Arts, so at least the balance is there!

If we return now to the Sun, and look at Gematria, we see that the number for the Sun is 666. This number is positive and represents the active charge of Solar energy, associated with masculinity. The number 1080 however, is receptive and passive and is connected with the Moon, water, intuition, and femininity.

> Radius of the Moon in miles: 1080
>
> Number of stanzas in *"Rig-Veda"* 1080
>
> Number of beads on a Hindu rosary 1080
>
> Number of bricks in an Indian Fire Altar 1080
>
> The phrase *"Spirit of Earth"* 1080
>
> The phrase *"Fountain of Wisdom"* 1080

1080 is ying and 666 is yang.

The number of a grain of mustard seed, (reputed to be the missing final piece on the Great Pyramid) 1746 (666+1080) 1746 is the number of fusion, representing the union between the two opposite principles of Nature. The phrase *"The Spirit of the World"* = 1746.

According to the old Alchemists, life was created by the fusion of two elements, Mercury and Sulphur. The first is female and passive, the second is male and active. In the old numerical philosophy, the numbers of these two elements were Mercury 1080 and Sulphur 666.

I demonstrated in *"Celtic Lore"* how the square with the odd words like a cross word, when changed to numbers showed the passage of the Sun and also the number 72. It also showed the Great Year and so forth. I will not repeat it here, but it does show how important the Sun was to these earlier people,

74

it would have played a major part in their Rituals and presumably was of paramount importance in their daily lives, their myths and fables and so forth. Religious symbolism is closely linked to the *"Age"* in which that particular philosophy flourishes.

According to the ancients, the material Sun is but a reflection/reflector of the Spiritual Sun, which is the source of life; i.e. the Logos who is the emanation from the Creator/Creatrix. The physical Universe is receptive, a realm of *Effects*. The unseen, spiritual realm is the sphere of *Cause*. The soul or intellectual realm, is the realm of mediation. (Similar to the Druids threes again, of active, passive and reconciling neutral). Jesus was a mediator, and when he said,*"no man cometh to the Father but by me"*, he was voicing a philosophical truth that pre-dated him by thousands of years. He was just the last in a long line of Seer-Prophets.

Mankind also has this threefold nature, physical, emotional, and mental. This again is a reflection of our Spiritual nature, also three fold. The symbol for these two sets of threes, is the six pointed star, the two triangles being interwoven. That the Hebrews were aware of the importance of this Sigil there can be no doubt. But it most certainly pre-dated them and their use of it.

If one looks at the procession of the Great Years, before the Piscean Age was the Arian Age, before that the Taurean. So the Bull was sacred, then the Ram then the Fish. Jesus must have been alive at the time of the change from sheep to fish. He used the lamb as a symbol, but not as much as those who had gone before him had done. The Old Testament is full of sheep and lambs. The priests were called *"Shepherds"*, in the Arian Age and lambs were a sacrificial animal. The early Christians had the fish as their symbol not long after the crucifixion. So, as we are gradually now changing into the *"Age of Aquarius"*, round about the birth of Jesus the Age was changing from Ram to Fishes. It would follow therefore, that from about 4000 B.C., to 2000 B.C., was the Age of Taurus.

There is a pitfall however when looking at legends in this way, and that is when one comes to the emphasis on leonine symbols and influence. For example, Hercules and Samson are two semi-mythical heroes with leonine connotations. The emphasis on matters leonine however, are not concerned with the Zodiacal Ages, but are related to the Sun. One clue to this, lies in the story of Samson and his loss of power when his hair was cut. Ages ago, the Druids say that when the Sun was losing its power in the Autumn, they saw the shrinking of the Suns rays as hair diminishing, and the ordinary folk used to cut off their hair and throw it into a river in a kind of sympathy act with the Sun.

That Freemasonry has old and venerable roots is demonstrated by their symbol of seven stars at the upper end of the Sacred Ladder. These are the Pleiades, found in the constellation of Taurus - the Bull. In Zoroastra's Chamber of Initiation, the Sun was depicted emerging from the back of Taurus.

There are writings concerning Osiris which state that he was away from his country bringing illumination to other peoples when he was slain. This confirms in my opinion, that he was a Sun God, the Sun illuminating many peoples as it crosses the sky.

To return for a moment to the Zodiacal Ages, it would seem that the emphasis in the distant past of various animals in succession, is an indication primarily of the particular Zodiacal Age in which events took place, or were purported to have taken place.

This can be tested in some instances:- The Minoan civilisation on the island of Crete had been establ-ished and flourished many years prior, say to 2000 BC. That these people had a philosophy based on bull worship, is an established provable fact.

A final look at Sun Gods; Serapsis, the Alexandrian god, may have been the model from which early christians got the idea of how Jesus looked. Some writers have seen Serapsis as the prototype of Christ. Serapsis became the supreme deity of both the Egyptians and the Greeks, until about 350 A.D.

Richard Payne Knight wrote that Serapsis was worshipped at Samothrace. Also that Osiris, Mithras and the Phoenician Adonis, were one and the same, i.e. Serapsis. This is stated in a hymn to the Sun, composed by Matrianus Capella, the writer and composer. (Circa 400 A.D.).

The Norse Odhinnic Mysteries were no different in theme from those of the Mediterranean and Egypt. In the Odhinnic Rites, the Neophyte was given the task of raising Baldur from the dead. In fact, the Neophyte unknowingly played the part of Baldur the Beautiful. He passed through caverns which symbolised the worlds and spheres of nature. The Priests who were his Initiators represented the Sun, Moon and Stars.

Eventually the Neophyte was guided to a room where stood a statue of Baldur. The chamber roof was lined with shields, and a plant growing there had seven blooms on it, symbolising the seven Planets. The chamber represented the House of Wisdom. The Neophyte took his oaths on a bared sword blade. He drank mead from a cup made from a human skull. He was given a ring to identify him, and was hailed as being re-born. It was said that he had died and been re-born, without passing through the gates of death.

The Eleusian Mysteries again had similar aims and objectives. The Lesser and Greater Mysteries, were both based on the number nine, i.e. 9 days of Initiation, passing through nine spheres to descend into the World of Matter, and so on.

The Greater Mysteries were concluded by the (Sanscrit?) words *"Konx Om Pax"*, which phrase will be familiar to Qabalists and Freemasons alike. The Candidate entered the Initiatory process unclothed, representing the concept that they were not yet clad in the true knowledge. They were then given animal skin to wear and later on, a consecrated robe. The Candidate passed through two gates, the first one led downward and symbolised earthly birth and ignorance. The second gate led upward into a brightly lit chamber.

The legend of Tammuz is probably the oldest known legend of a dying and resurrected god; it is certainly earlier than 3000 B.C. Tammuz is referred to as a *"Shepherd"*, or *"Lord of the Shepherd Flock"*. The resurrection of Tammuz was accompanied by celebration, the people now calling him *"their Redeemer"*. I would think that Tammuz was originally a foliate or vegetation god, in view of the legend we have of him, where he descended into the Underworld and Ishtar went to seek him. His importance as a god must also overlap to some degree, the change of the Zodiacal *"Age"*, although we cannot be sure now, when one age commenced and another ended.

That Tammuz still had a following during the last Millennia of the pre-Christian era, is evident from the Old Testament, where it mentions that the people were weeping for Tammuz. All we know for sure, is that each Sign of the Zodiac was taken to be thirty degrees in duration. (72 years x 30 degrees = 2160).

The Mysteries of Adonis which took place in Egypt, Byblos and Phoenicia, again have this theme of resurrection. *"Adonis"* or *"Adonai"* simply means *"Lord"*, and was presumably applied to the Sun as representative of a Sun/Solar god. The Jews adopted the name of Adonai as an overt name for their deity. Adonis was born on the 25th December, as are *all* magical or deified children.

In *"The Golden Bough"*, Frazer says,

> *"Bethlehem, the traditionary birthplace of the Lord, was shaded by a grove of still older Syrian Lord, Adonis, and that where the infant Jesus had wept, the lover of Venus was bewailed"*.

After three days in the tomb, Adonis rises on the 25th day of March, while the priests exclaim, *"he is risen"* !

Adonis was born out of a Myrrh tree. Most writers are of the opinion that Adonis was originally a vegetation god. In Phrygia at one time there was apparently a school of religious philosophy, which concerned itself solely with the life, death and resurrection of the god known to them as *"Atys"*, who in the opinion of some, was the same god as Adonis. Atys was born at midnight on 24th December, in common with other supernatural children, and died by either being gored as was Adonis, or by castrating himself under a pine tree. If the species of Pine were known to us, it would then perhaps be possible to see the hidden symbolism of this act.

The Great Mother who at this period of time and location was named Cybele, took his body and put it in a cave. Atys was in his tomb for three days, and resurrected at the time of the old Fertility Rites, in other words, at Easter. By his death and resurrection he overcame death for all of his Initiates. The Rites of Atys included a sacred meal, at which his Initiates ate from a drum and drank from a cymbal.

Cybele took the Pine tree with her, as the immortality of Atys had also been given to the tree. That the Sun represents the male deity not that the male deity is a representation of the Sun, I hope is clear.

The Sun rises and sets, it also has its yearly path through the sky and the Signs of the Zodiac.

The Druids and Shamanistic Priests did not worship the Sun, only the active masculine, generative principle, that it symbolised.

So what of the Moon?

Well that was the greatest mystery of all, paramount in all old beliefs. Often not spoken of in the company of non Initiates, as it is the female, passive, receptive principle, (also triune like the god, but extended to nine-fold), and what the Moon symbolised was held in great awe. The Moon Tides were reproduced within the female body. As the Earth refreshed by water, (female also), and warmed by the Sun's rays, (male), gave forth life, so did woman. It is possible that the *"Yods"* falling from the Moon in the Rider-Waite Tarot deck, may depict *"Moon-Dew"*. In the realm of human beings, this is the awesome menstrual flow, generally coinciding with the Dark Moon time.

In conclusion; religious symbolism is closely allied to the *"Age"* in which that particular philosophy flourished. Manly Hall states that Scorpio as a serpent, was often used by the ancients to symbolise wisdom, which could be why Christians are taught that the serpent is evil. (The Sign of Scorpio has three creatures allied to it. The scorpion, the snake and the Eagle). If one follows what has been said regarding the reflection of the sun's rays into a particular Sign, then when the Arian Age is mentioned, it is really also concerned with Libra and Libran balance. So the Piscean Age when the Sun was actually in Virgo, would account for the importance given to the Mother of Jesus, and why she was depicted as a virgin. It would all have been allegorical and full of symbolism. All it meant was that he was born in the Age of Virgo the virgin.

In the Aquarian Age then, a great leonine influence should be evident, which is probably why the comment is made in regard to some occult paths, that Initiation by the *"Grip of the Lions Paw"*, will once again be celebrated. This phrase is also used in esoteric Freemasonry, so they too are evidently aware of the correct method to employ when referring to Zodiacal Ages. The *"Lion Grip"*, is also an ancient Eastern name for one way of demonstrating the Sign for *"Air"*, using the hands. Aquarius is of course, an *"Air"* sign in the Zodiac.

As I mentioned the sun's rays diminishing and being observed as hair, I thought I would explain the source of this, and also enlarge on it somewhat. It is from a book written last century, by a Christian Druid, and the book is called, *"The Light of Britannia"*. The author was named *"Morien O Morgan"*.

I will quote here from the book: *"The British Druids"* which compared the annual journey of the sun to the duration of human life.

"He is "born" at the winter solstice, and begins his career as a child called Hu Gadarn. The personified sun drops his title at the vernal equinox and assumes the new title of Tegid. Tegid signifies All Beautiful, and the title is retained until the summer solstice when he is in the full effulgence of his strength. Between the summer solstice and autumn equinox he begins to decay, and comes to be called Tegid Voel, or Bald-All-Beautiful, in reference to the suns rays beginning to diminish in strength and quantity, the rays being compared to hair. The sun now enters upon the period of old age and decrepitude. He is now called by divers names or titles, namely, Dyvnwawl Moelmud (Sombre Light, Bald and Dumb); Arawn (slow, or to wait); Said-Wrn (Saturn). Another title of the sun, in his full strength, is Arthur, or Arddir (gardener or husbandman), and he is the husbandman of the Earth - the Garden. The same applies also to the

variety of titles given by the Druids to the earth during the year.

Thus, the three Queens of Arthur (the sun), are described Morgwen la Fai (the earth in spring); the second is said to be the Queen of North Wales (the earth in summer); the third, the Queen of the Desert Places (the earth in winter). Gwenwyver corresponds with Flora. The name is a compound of three words: Gwen (Holy), Wy (Water) and Mer muted to Ver (Essence).

The whole compound signifies Holy-Water-Essence, meaning the sap of the earth streaming up in vegetation and trees under the influence of the heat left in the atmosphere at night......"

The reader should bear in mind that the author was a Christian Druid, of a revivalist group, and that while these meanings are valid, they are only at a very probationary level, before even the Bardic. It is the same with all the Mystery philosophies, the veils before the knowledge are taken away by degrees, not all at once!

Talismans, Bind Runes and the Coelbren

A Talisman does not have to be specially made. It can be some particular piece of jewellery, or a keepsake that has a special meaning for the owner, or that the owner considers is lucky for them. If this is the case, then all you have to do, is consecrate it and mentally imbue it as a Talisman, for whatever purpose you wish it to have, even just as a general *"good-luck"* charm.

It is a bit like a Hag Stone in reverse! However, if you wish to make a Talisman for a particular purpose, one of the simplest ways of making one, is with handicraft clay that can be baked in an ordinary oven.

Choose a colour for the clay that you consider appropriate. The clay can be moulded quite easily by hand, so a small flattish disc is the simplest to make. You can pierce it with a knitting needle before baking, so that it can be worn like a pendant, on a piece of leather thonging or a chain, or you can just keep it in a handbag or pocket, in which case you may prefer to make a small *"pebble"* shape.

Once it is baked, symbols can be painted on it with either a fine brush or a sketching pen. Of course, if you wish, you can include in the clay something you feel will help it to work. Either from yourself, such as a small piece of your hair, or a particular herb or dried flower, it is entirely up to you what you think should be in i t- if anything.

The painted symbol should indicate the Talismans role for you. Once it is finished, it can be passed three times through incense smoke, or fire smoke, while you state the reason for its manufacture. One this is completed, no one but yourself should handle it.

A Bind Rune is an effective and simple talismanic symbol of intent. I will list some here to give a few ideas for them.

Bind Rune for protection

Bind Rune for better health

Bind Rune for success

Bind Rune for enlightenment

These can be consecrated at certain hours for a Planetary influence to be invoked, and a bit farther on, I list the Planetary hours for each day of the week and for a 24 hour period.

The incense you pass the Talisman through if you are not using fire smoke, (a Circle fire), would depend on what the Talisman was for. If using the fire, you would burn suitable and appropriate herbs or a herb on that. If you are using an object already in your possession, then the consecration would be the same, except you would pass it through water also. Clay has earth and water already in it, smoke can be looked on as fire and air.

If the Talisman is for the family and is really for the house, then you can consecrate it where it stands if outside and large. Some people I know have a stone dragon near the front door for example, while another friend has carved, wooden gnomes as door or gate wards. These can be done at purchase, and as they are located in the place where they are going to *"live"* !

The *"Coelbren"* are also known as *"Omen Stones"* at the present time; they are a Celtic set of Runes, but they are Welsh not Irish or Scottish, as the name implies. They are twenty two of the Runes that are listed in the Welsh book *"Barddas"*. The complete set of forty were used as an alphabet, but these twenty two, can be used for Divination. I list them here, with their Welsh and English names, and also their spiritual interpretation, rather than the mundane.

There are many sets of Runes and other divinatory tools, which can be used for guiding in the physical world, but these are mainly concerned with inner development, although they can be used as an alternative to perhaps the Tarot for ordinary meanings. The English for each Rune is a Tree as in Ogham.

Llwyafen Elm tree
Symbol:

Long "A" Well Being, fellowship, happiness, goodwill.

Alilim Fir tree
Symbol:

"A" Container/contained. Increase of active/passive powers. Transformer, expressor of spiritual power and knowledge. Allied to the Moon, the Great Mother and is a symbol of birth.

Bedwen Birch tree
Symbol:

"B" Birth and cycle of life. The creative process, movement, works of protection. Opening out as of buds.

Collen Hazel tree
Symbol:

"C" Regeneration, ability love, honour, mankind. The making of three from two. Music.

Derwen Oak tree
Symbol:

"D" Light, polarity. The reception of mystical wisdom. Spiritual strength. Synthesis of the powers of night and day.

Aethnen Aspen tree
Symbol:

"E" Trust, loyalty, fertility, swiftness. Prophetic wisdom.

Gwernen Alder tree
Symbol:

"F" Mobile force, energy, becoming. Strengthens psychic ability.

Eiddew Ivy tree
Symbol:

"G" Magical force, giving, harmony. Mystical union.

Ceccysen Reeds
Symbol:

"Ng" Potential energy, gestation, centreing, energy releases.

Draenen-Wen Hawthorn tree
Symbol:

"H" Protection, completion, numinous knowledge. Associated with the White Goddess.

Ywen Yew tree
Symbol:

"I" Endurance, vision, Initiation into wisdom.

Cerddinen Rowan tree
Symbol:

"L" Primal water. Passage. Growth. Guidance. Basic life energy.

Miaren Vine
Symbol:

"M" Generosity, faithfulness, comfort, well-being.

Onnen Ash tree
Symbol:

"N" Resistance, deliverance. Inspiration. Concept of stepping forth into manifestation. Overcoming negativity.

Eithinen Gorse
Symbol:

"O" Comfort in the material world. Generosity. Faithfulness.

Gwyddfid Honeysuckle
Symbol:

"P" Cause and effect. Change, perception, ideas.

Afallen Apple tree
Symbol:

"Q" Life-giving force. Mode by which that life is sustained.
Ysgawen

Elder tree
Symbol:

"R" Ritual. Rhythm. Access to inner advice. Archetypal law
and order.

Helygen Willow tree
Symbol:

"S" Will, honour, success. Associated with the Dark Isis and
Lustral water.

Celywnen Holly tree
Symbol:

"T" Justice.World order. Spiritual discipline. Order through
balance.

Grug Heather
Symbol:

"*U*" Wisdom, health, vital strength. Healing, inspiration. Origins and destiny.

Uchelwydd Mistletoe
Symbol:

"*Y*" Reward, fruition, peace, creativity. Enlightenment.

Here is a little rhyme or couple of verses, that pertain to Runes when using them for Divination:

> *Mark the Guardians of the Signs,*
> *Know them well, for they will prove,*
> *All the Light and Dark of Fate*
> *As the Weaver moves the loom.*
>
> *The Pattern cannot altered be,*
> *But the knots may be undone;*
> *A smoother Pattern marked for Thee,*
> *Who from the Stones has knowledge rung.*

There are two ways of reading these Runes, one is to take nine from the bag without looking then read all nine, or cast them on a table, and read those which are face up. If you read nine you can place them in a straight line as they are taken from the bag, and read them from right to left.

The other way is to lay them still in a straight line, but in groups of three. The right hand set being then the past, the middle one the present and the left hand trio the future.

Another method is to utilise the *"Rune-Row"*, but only have seven Runes, and lay them as follows:

RUNES

6   5   4   3   2   1

Rune 7

Runes 1 and 2 are the problem,

Runes 3 and 4 are outside factors,

Runes 5 and 6 the Rune-Row answer,

Rune 7 is the final outcome which will eventuate from the solution.

The Ancient Book of Appin

There is an ancient book which belonged to the MacGregor family of Scotland and which has now been lost or mislaid. It was translated from Latin and Celtic languages into English some time in the distant past. Only fragments from this ancient book are still in the possession of some family members. I include it as a matter of interest. The book was known as: *"MacGregors of Appin Book of Wisdom"*.

The Laws

Here be the Laws : the Law was ordained of Old:

> 1. Treat others as you desire to be treated. Speak them fair. Kind words are as Pearls. Evil words are Swords.

> 2. Should another do you wickedness, do not seek revenge or return evil for evil. That which you do wrong destroys the Spirit. If others do *you* wrong *they* will pay the price. For.......

> 3. The Evil you do another rebounds upon you threefold.

> 4. Never use your knowledge selfishly-for material gain, sex or to harm another. Use it for the help and good of all.

> 5. If by an action of yours, another is *seriously* harmed-beware-if you are not repaid for your crime in *this* life, it will be *thrice* in the next.

6. *Never* accept money for using your Art. Money often smears the character. You are but *"human".* You may be weak, and become corrupt and take more than you can give.

7. Never threaten. Never say you wish ill of anyone.

8. Animals and birds are our brothers. Do not abuse them:- even plants are living things. Kill only for food or in self-defence: not for *"sport"*.

9. Should you receive many unexpected gifts, money or great crops or other good things; share with another, for the law saeth *"Give that ye may receive"*. Should you become selfish or grasping, you will find your ability to *"receive"* will become less.

10. If another should use the Craft to do you harm, it is lawful to *"reverse the flow"*, this and this *only*. *Do not* seek further (extra) revenge from *spite*. Nor is it lawful to cast a curse.

11. You *"own"* nothing: All you have is *"lent"*. *Knowledge* is your only *true* possession. Use it wisely and justly. It is all you take *with* you from life to life. The material possessions become the property of another. Your physical body eventually becomes nothing.

12. Do not try to impress others with your knowledge. Most are not ready. They will think you boast or are mad. You know what you know. You can do what you can do. Why *need* tell another? Discussion between trusted friends is permissible.

13. Do nothing you *know* to be wrong; others may consider you wise and good. If you know yourself to be weak and evil (though none *other* may know) you will grow to hate and despise yourself.

I have no way of knowing whether this is in fact a genuine fragment from the past, but it seems to be and anyway, it has very good sense in it!

There is a lady at present still alive although very old, who is of the MacGregor Clan, and she claims to have first hand knowledge of this fragmentary old book, I see no reason to doubt her.

Back To Allegory !

Looking at the old tales again for a moment, there are some hints on what is *really* being talked about, in strangeness of behaviour, or rather puzzling incidents.

I believe I have stated elsewhere that the Druids in particular, and the Celts in general, worked with nine psychic centres or chakras. Initially they teach there are nine of these, and although they are usually awakened initially from one to nine, there are other methods which in some instances help with light trance work. In this instance, the numbers are worked in the sequence of three, six, and nine, and then one, four, two, eight, five, seven. (I have mentioned this sequence of numbers before, with reference to the Enneagram, which can also be a working symbol, allied to the human body).

The knowledge of this method, signifies some degree of skill in the practitioner. The very first time I ever tried it, after the 3,6,9, sequence, I got extremely dizzy! I could not continue at that time with the others either. It was of course, because I was not experienced enough at the time with the Psychic Centre work, to try this out, but as a younger person, lack of knowledge had never deterred me greatly!

In the Irish book *"The Tain"*, the champion Cuchulain juggles nine apples as a Warrior feat. We all know apples have magical connotations, but there is still nothing very remarkable going on, unless he is demonstrating his prowess in *"juggling"* the Psychic Centres in a difficult way.

It would then make more sense; particularly when one comes across this type of reference to nine things in other systems For example: There is a Ritual in the Anglo-Saxon *"Lacnunga"* where a corn spirit has taken a woman's soul, and the Sorcerer is chanting during the Ritual, to retrieve it.

He chants:

> *"Corn Spirit I have you,*
> *my fangs pierce your flesh*
> *your battle armour is rent and torn,*
> *your nine layers will be stripped,*
> *and when the last is put to flames,*
> *the woman's soul will be free."*

He then tears ears of corn chanting:

> "Nine were Corn Spirits layers,
> Nine layers of Power,
> Nine were the links of armour,
> But nine now I lower, nine becomes eight."

He goes on, eight becoming seven and so on until he has ended the Power of the Corn Spirit. It seems obvious to me that it is his *Psychic Power* that he is using and also that he is battling against. Incidentally, this quote is from a marvellous book by Brian Bates, called *"The Way of Wyrd"*.

The Caers in *"The Spoils Of Annwn"* are as I said earlier, also related to the Psychic Centres, the Castle of Sloping or Shelving Sides, being the Solar Plexus Centre, and the sides are the rib cage.

In the *"Song of Amergin"* where Amergin is battling Mil for supremacy, many of the lines apply to the Oghams, and therefore also to the Psychic Centres.

A Rite of Warding in a Circle

This little Ritual is to protect and ward off when working, if you feel or know that there may be others not very much in sympathy with your Circle Tradition, that may either physically or perhaps psychically, attempt to interfere or intervene in your Working area.

You cast the Circle, then place a little mound of rock or sea salt in each quarter. You trace the Sigil of Oenghus in each quarter in place of whatever other symbol you may normally use. You then go to each quarter in turn, starting in the East, and declaim:

> *"I call on the God of Light to Ward and to keep all safe that here do stand."*

The herbs to be burnt are, *Dandelion, Rosemary* and *Mugwort.* A Yarrow Wand should be placed in the North on commencement.

Here is the Sigil of Oenghus:

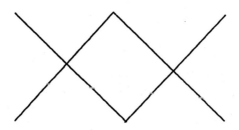

An Esbat in the Scottish Isles ?

A very dear friend in America, sent me an extremely interesting Ritual. Not only was the content fascinating, but so was the manner in which she came by it. I reproduce it here, exactly as it was sent to me, including her Copyright, her name and her address:

In the course of some past-life recovery work, some images emerged which I had the impression represented Scottish Witches on an island in the Orkneys, or it may have been the Hebrides. Whether these images came from an actual past-life experience of my own or not, I am not prepared to swear; but some features are so interesting that I would like to share them.

We came on shaggy ponies and on foot, by forest paths, and met at a glade deep in the forest, just as the Moon was becoming visible above the treetops. As soon as all had arrived and all needful articles were set in order, the first thing we did was gather in an old-fashioned football-type huddle.

We made the circle small and tight with our arms across each other's waists and shoulders. Our heads we inclined toward the centre until they touched all around. We began a deep-throated hum, very low at first. Its purpose was to mentally burrow into a state of intense concentration, meanwhile attuning to one another. There were words in the chant, but I couldn't catch either the words or the meaning, if any. I felt that the syllables may have been for the value of the sound, and may have had no left-brain meaning.

Then there were the knives. An article of traditional masculine Highland dress is the "sgian dubh" (literally, "black knife".) This is a small but business-like black-handled knife, carried in a sheath which is tucked into the garter which holds up the Highlander's right stocking, just below the knee. (This is of course, the natural place for any ribbon or string to be tied on the leg, and is the way garters are worn by the little dancing figures in European cave paintings. A garter worn above the knee is absurd. It impeded circulation and keeps falling down.) All these Witches, male and female, wore the "sgian dubh" in just that manner. We wore the ordinary dress of the day, which looked to me like the Elizabethan or Jacobean period. The women hoisted their petticoats to reach the knives. I got a sense that at this epoch it was considered "unladylike", even immodest, for women to wear them.

We employed these knives as we now do our Arddames. I saw an interesting use of the knives in an energy-raising dance. This was a very energetic, light-footed leaping circlewise dance, done to pipe music. At intervals, the dancers would rush into the centre and clash their upraised knives in a particular way, producing a ringing metallic swish, like that you hear when Morris dancers snatch their blades out of sword-lock.

To get such a prolonged sound out of such short blades, it was necessary to swirl the blades together as they were drawn apart. Then the dancers whirled away from the centre and with a whoop lunged outwards, thrusting their knives ahead of them. They held this posture for a beat or two, then took up the circle dance again. A strong drumbeat cued the figures of the dance.

I gather that this figure was meant to unite the energies of the knives and boost their power by contact with one another. Each clash boosted the power another notch. The sharp sound was to summon spirits (Air elementals?) The outward lunge was of course to repel unwanted forces, an affirmation of the Witches' sovereignty within their space and of their ability to defend it.

Wherever these images came from, the ritual elements seem very effective to me. If you try them, I would like to hear from you how they worked out.

Blessed be,

Erinna Northwind
17 West Baltimore St. #17
Lynn, Mass.01902
U.S.A.

I have not yet had the opportunity to try this out, but to me it has the *"feel"* of the genuine article. I have had letter and phone contact with Erinna for over five years, and have great respect for her as a person, and as a witch. I feel personally, that it may be Orkney Craft, or maybe it was one method on Callanish?

Callanish as far as I know, has never been looked at very closely from a Craft point of view. Personally I have never been there, something I much regret, as there are many lines of standing stones there apparently, and no one seems to have done much research of the island. Of course, now living on the other side of the world, I may be very much out of date; in which case, I would greatly appreciate any information I could get, on the findings.

If any reader knows of books or articles on Callanish, I would very much like to hear from them. Scottish Craft per se does seem to be a very neglected area although I believe it is extremely active. I know there is a strong Druidic Path still alive and well in Scotland.

Planetary Ruler for Each Hour of the Day and the Night....

One hour after sunrise-hours of the day

	MON.	TUES.	WED.	THURS.	FRI.	SAT.
1.	Moon	Mars	Mercury	Jupiter	Venus	Saturn
2.	Saturn	Sun	Moon	Mars	Mercury	Jupiter
3.	Jupiter	Venus	Saturn	Sun	Moon	Mars
4.	Mars	Mercury	Jupiter	Venus	Saturn	Sun
5.	Sun	Moon	Mars	Mercury	Jupiter	Venus
6.	Venus	Saturn	Sun	Moon	Mars	Mercury
7.	Mercury	Jupiter	Venus	Saturn	Sun	Moon
8.	Moon	Mars	Mercury	Jupiter	Venus	Saturn
9.	Saturn	Sun	Moon	Mars	Mercury	Jupiter
10.	Jupiter	Venus	Saturn	Sun	Moon	Mars
11.	Mars	Mercury	Jupiter	Venus	Saturn	Sun
12.	Sun	Moon	Mars	Mercury	Jupiter	Venus

SUNDAY: Hours of the day:

1. Sun
2. Venus
3. Mercury
4. Moon
5. Saturn
6. Jupiter
7. Mars
8. Sun
9. Venus
10. Mercury
11. Moon
12. Saturn

One hour after sunset: hours of the night:

	MON.	TUES.	WED.	THURS.	FRI.	SAT.
1.	Venus	Saturn	Sun	Moon	Mars	Mercury
2.	Mercury	Jupiter	Venus	Saturn	Sun	Moon
3.	Moon	Mars	Mercury	Jupiter	Venus	Saturn
4.	Saturn	Sun	Moon	Mars	Mercury	Jupiter
5.	Jupiter	Venus	Saturn	Sun	Moon	Mars
6.	Mars	Mercury	Jupiter	Venus	Saturn	Sun
7.	Sun	Moon	Mars	Mercury	Jupiter	Venus
8.	Venus	Saturn	Sun	Moon	Mars	Mercury
9.	Mercury	Jupiter	Venus	Saturn	Sun	Moon
10.	Moon	Mars	Mercury	Jupiter	Venus	Saturn
11.	Saturn	Sun	Moon	Mars	Mercury	Jupiter
12.	Jupiter	Venus	Saturn	Sun	Moon	Mars

SUNDAY: Hours of the night:

1. Jupiter
2. Mars
3. Sun
4. Venus
5. Mercury
6. Moon
7. Saturn
8. Jupiter
9. Mars
10. Sun
11. Venus
12. Mercury

I have included these hours, because sometimes it can be very important to be working at a particular time when a certain Planet is in its Hour, in order to assist you.

Working on the Inner Planes

Some Advice, Guidance and Wisdoms Learned

As readers of my previous books know, for many years now I have had one main contact during Meditation, or working on the Inner Planes as it is generally called. This Archetype identified to me as *"The Myrddin"*. This is the title of a particular Archetype, who is now known to many people as *"Merlin"*, although that is not his name, it is his title, as I explained in *"Celtic Lore & Druidic Ritual"*. *"Myrddin"* is simply the older Welsh spelling of that title.

So the following are all experiences I have had, when contacting The Myrddin through the *"Glass Tower Rite"*.

One little homily I discovered a few years ago, I think sums up this type of learning experience, and it is this:

> Meditation is *listening,* as opposed to *praying* which is *talking"*.

So here are some of the Inner Planes Journeys:

The Myrddin speaks,

> *"Always there must be balance; in people and in the Universe. If the scales tip too far one way, then a greater*

than equal weight must be placed to bring them back to equilibrium ".

In the broadest sense the way the world has been tipping farther and farther one way. It has gone on for so long that now a great weight must be placed on the other side of the scale to restore equanimity. The problem with the human race is that they themselves are out of balance - "out of true" is a more significant phrase than is generally realised. They are no longer "true". They are also so out of alignment from within, that most of them cannot imagine being any other way. In one sense they are sick. The Planet itself is sick.

Now, man wishes to infect the stars. Mankind is like a being living in the dark, who was told long ago about the light. But now it is an unreal concept. He no longer even believes in the light. Man has become almost a two dimensional being. His world has become smaller and smaller until now he believes that happiness consists of filling this small, dark place with "things". He has lost all concept of higher realms, in fact he does not even really see his own domain - the Planet Earth. It is just something to be pillaged in order to give him more "things". He rushes blindly from one sterile place to another, always seeking this strange goal called "happiness", which always eludes him. He is terrified of death, seeing it as the end of possessing "things".

Happiness is not a commodity that one can order by quantity or weight. Happiness is boundless like the ocean. But like the ocean, no one has ownership to it. Happiness is within a balanced being. Happiness is fitting into the Universe, almost without the realisation that it is occurring.

Some people know their life is wrong. Some realise what is happening, but in their desire to learn and correct the balance in themselves, they have spawned a whole new group of shallow people. They do not appear to be shallow, they are self proclaimed wise ones, some even claim to be "Masters". But they are no better than the greedy men in the dark, busily collecting "things".

In some ways these masters are worse. For they claim to have the knowledge that will lead those seeking balance, into the light and into a sense of equilibrium. But they will only impart their knowledge for a price. They also, are collectors of "things", only theirs, apart from money, are intangible "things" that feed their pride and vanity.

Be quiet and still.

Walk in gardens.

Walk in open empty places.

Listen to the sea or a running brook.

Watch a bird in flight.

Quieten the mind,

Feel the Universe,

Look at the starry sky.

This is the way to equilibrium. Do not sit in a crowded room, on a chair which has been bought for an evening by you, listening to one of those "enlightened ones". They count their success in money and esteem.

What is enlightened in that?

Each human being has the means within themselves to feel the still, quiet centre of being which denotes harmony. A little flower has more to tell you of harmony and awareness of harmony, than the greatest self-proclaimed master".

On another visit, I was shown a plain, clear glass ball, rather like an old fishing float.

The Myrddin said:

> *"If you hold it in a certain way in the sunlight, the sun puts a rainbow prism in the glass."*

I took the glass ball and found that by standing in a certain spot, and holding the ball at a particular angle, the sun's rays did make a rainbow of colour in the ball.

When The Myrddin saw that I had found the colours, he took the glass ball from me, smiled gently and said;

> *"Nevertheless, it is only a plain glass ball. You cannot stand forever transfixed, holding it at just that angle, in order to make it look as if it was full of rainbow colours. It is a plain glass ball and must be accepted as that, and appreciated for its simple plainness."*

I took this little episode to apply to life, as a reminder to appreciate what one has, even if it is not as exciting or as colourful as one would wish.

Another time:

The Myrddin speaks:

> *"Before all else is the breath. Breathing correctly is very important to the physical, metal and spiritual well-being of mankind. Breath is the link with the Infinite. Clean air is vital. Go into a place of clean air and breathe! Deep breaths fill the lungs, calm the mind and replenish the spirit. Man was not made to live in dirt and noise.*

Man was made to live where he can hear a tree breathe. Man's body was made to walk on grass, to climb over rocks, to wade through water. All so called civilisation is destructive to mankind."

And again:

"Good is not an absence of evil. Good is an active state. Evil is not an abstraction. It exists solely in the physical realm of humanity. A Lion pulls down a Gazelle, that is not evil. It is the instinct of the Lion to kill to eat, it is the fatalism of the Gazelle to be killed for food. But man can reason, if a man slays another creature wantonly that is evil. Only in man does evil manifest.

A Mother may slay an intruder in blind panic to protect her little child. The intruder has brought the evil with him. His evil intent has rebounded onto him. The power of love is the greatest force in the physical world. Perfect love is unselfish. Perfect love is uplifting. Whether it is one human for another, for another living creature other than mankind, or love of a human soul for unseen Guardians of the physical realm. Love freely given is its own reward, indifference is the first small step on the path to evil. Indifference is an absence of emotion or feeling; it is better to feel too much - to have too much emotion than to be indifferent.

Indifference has brought the Planet Earth to its parlous state. Beware of smugness. Do not spend so much time on what you consider to be your spiritual development, that you neglect your loved ones. That is not spirituality, that is selfishness.

Remember the Path of the Hearth-Fire. It is the most satisfying Path of all for a normal human soul. The complete aesthete is a very rare being, and is it right and proper for a physical plane soul, to sever all contact with the physical realm? One is in a physical world for a reason. To participate, enjoy, learn and perhaps to assist others to grow in their Inner Self, is a balanced aim for all members of the human race. But beware of trying to force your knowledge on another, each individual grows in a different way.

The Path that you tread, may not be the correct Path for another. There are many ways that lead to the ultimate Truth. Indeed, there are many interpretations of the Ultimate Truth for the human soul. Do not be loud in voicing the knowledge you have obtained. It is enough that you are aware that you are treading the balanced way. If someone asks for guidance then give it - but not in vanity or from a sense of self- importance.

Do not confuse the dark with what is evil or bad. Without the dark there is no light, always there must be balance. Consider the purest flower, a Snowdrop perhaps, or a White Rose; it blows in the gentle breeze, the clear sky shines on it. But its life-blood, its very essence is deep in the dark earth. T

he beauty that glows in the Sun, would not be without the dark. Both Sun and Moon give light in the dark. Sometimes we need the full glow of sunlight to shine in the dark corners we are fearful of, for then we will see that those shadowy places contain nothing but dust or cobwebs.

When we are sure of our place in the scheme of things however, we can stand in the gentle Moonlight and know we are not threatened by those dark corners.

Mankind has forgotten the Silver Web. It covers and is part of, this Universe. All things are part of it. The human race should fit with nature, nature and the Planet Earth are one with man. Why has he forgotten this? All are as one. Then all fits together harmoniously.

There are of course those who are aware of this and they are growing in number. All living things are of equal importance. Of course a human soul is different from a blade of grass or a tree, but in the natural order of things, they are different with different areas of usefulness, but of equal Importance

However, it is a gentle process to alter those who do not know this truth. Imagine a vast desert, barren and lifeless, but just here and there little clumps of green are sprouting. That is how it must be done. A few here and there who can see the terrible fate such a short distance away for this Planet. But imparting the knowledge of how to avert the outcome, to another few beings here and there who will listen, is like the little clumps of green in the desert. Gradually, gradually it will spread and grow.

Speak only to those who will listen and learn. Do not be disconsolate if their numbers are few. Remember the little bits of green. They will gradually combine and cover the barren waste. Do not despair when all seems dark. Remember, without the dark there can be no light. Always the middle way is the correct way, the path of balance and harmony.

A Mother who is too strict and overbearing becomes a tyrant. Her children know only fear, and will not grow in a happy and balanced manner. A Mother who, often through laziness, is over-indulgent and never checks or corrects, but always lets her children do whatever they wish, will also prevent them from growing in a happy and balanced manner. Always a middle path is the correct one to tread. It reconciles opposites, and achieves universal harmony. A little child is the wonder of the universe, a beautiful, unsullied miracle. Surely such a being deserves the best?

The best way is the middle way. A little child is a book with blank pages; make sure we turn this empty book into a wonderful illuminated manuscript, full of happy, wise, and harmonious thoughts for the future to read.

Try to see the pattern of which you are a small part. There is continuity in all life, which if lived harmoniously is for the ultimate good. Remember, you have chosen to be aware; you have chosen to learn. If you wished to live only on the material plane, gathering possessions, gaining worldly success, it may have been that your life would not have had tests and trials.

You would have gone blissfully like a worm in the dust, and have ended your days an undisturbed, contented worm, only aware of, and quite happy in, the dust. But you have chosen to ride Pegasus! Yes, you will be buffeted. Flung this way and that. But you have chosen to see above the treetops, above the mountain peaks. Your evolving is accelerated. So you have more wind tossing than the worm could even imagine!

But, if you hold fast, ride out the winds and storms, Pegasus will take you to those crystal turrets, which you have longed for you will achieve your hearts desire. Take pleasure in simple things. A butterfly is more beautiful than the coldest jewel in an empress' crown. Learn from simple things. They hold the keys to Universal knowledge.

Look at a Bee! He can fly because he knows that is what he was created for. He does not think:"I cannot do it! "It is impossible!" "I am too fat!" "My wings are too small!"

Sure of his place in the scheme of things - he flies! Look at a beehive. Ponder on those perfect, mystical, hexagonal shapes! What do they tell you? Geometry is the secret of the Universe - it is the magic of the Universe! Look at a crystal of quartz. Hold it and look! Look into the crystal and meditate. All is crystalline structure. A quartz crystal is a key to the Universe. It is the crown of the mineral kingdom-but it is more!

When all seems grey and hope is faint, gaze at a crystal and know it is the very essence of your being and the Universe. So, if you and the Universe are one, by this miracle of frozen light, how can you but rejoice and be cleansed. Full of the pure light of the Infinite."

One final episode; I was taken into an old barn. Rough wooden tables and benches were set out, the tables had wooden plates and mugs on them. I could smell hay. At the far end of the barn, was a big door through which came the sound of a fiddle, playing very old country music.

We went through the door. A lot of short, rather plump men and women were dancing a sort of round weaving dance. Their clothes were simple, but were of a style and period unknown to me. I was told by The Myrddin:

"They are celebrating the hay harvest. The grain harvest, which is more important, is yet to come and they do not know whether it will be good or bad, but that is in the future. They are celebrating what they have now. If the grain harvest is bad, they will says;

"Ah ! But think how good the hay was !"

If it is a good grain year, they will be doubly grateful. The main point is however, that they celebrate what they have now, and do not trouble themselves about the future."

There is one final journey I would like to mention although it did not concern The Myrddin directly. It made a great impression on me, and I include a poem I wrote about afterwards.

I was taken through a long mist-filled valley. At the far end, the land rose up in a steep incline. When I reached the top, it was a clear sunny early morning. The land was shaped a bit like a crescent Moon. In the curve of the horns was the sea or a lake, with the sun shining on it. One of the *"horns"* was farther round than the other. On this point of land, was a turreted castle, that shone like crystal. I was standing on soft grass, in what I can only describe as an orchard-garden.

There were old gnarled apple trees, but although they were laden with blossom, the air smelled of apples. Also the air was filled with soft music.

It was not like someone playing music, it was as if the air itself was musical. It was so peaceful and beautiful, that I did not want to leave, but was reminded kindly that I must do so. It was, as far as I can ascertain, the *"Apple Isle"*- Avalon. *"Avalon"* simply means *"Island of Apples"*, in the old speech.

Overleaf is the poem I wrote about this incident:

The Summerland

Through the valley mist shrouded
on Silverthorn the sure footed,
I rode out of time from the circles of Earth.
Up, up from the valley, to Fair Land of the Blest;
Sun filled was the Haven that greeted me gently,
air scented with apples, though snow-white
the blossoms, that crowded the branches
of Summerland trees.
I gazed at the Fair Land
that knows not cold winter.

Bewitched Crystal Castle gleamed in the sun.
Four turrets ablaze,
diamond bright in the morning,
reflected and shining on peaceful blue sea.
I stood with the Nine on brilliant greensward,
greeted by Myrddin, old faithful and wise.
The Hunter had shown me the Path through the valley,
but he told me not how soon my return.
Back to this Realm, faded and ailing
needing so much of Mankind's love and care.
But not for ever shall I linger
not for ever must I stay.
One bright golden morning the
Birds will call me,
Dark Guardian will lead me
back to my Home.
Back to the Fair Land heartbreakingly lovely,
Its air filled with soft music no man could invent.
Back to the peace of that Glorious Country,
A Heal-All for souls that are weary or lost.
One bright golden morning
The Birds will call me,
Dark Guardian will lead me
Back to my Home.

Learn This as if it Were a Law

1. Love all things in nature

2. Suffer no person to be harmed by deed or even thought. Thoughts vibrate into the Silver Web.

3. Go quietly and confidently among the ways and paths of the World.

4. Be mindful always of the Unseen Guardians.

5. Knowledge comes through application and the surety that the Universe will uphold and support you.

6. Contentment comes with knowing that a thread runs through your life, and all is for the ultimate good.

7. The truly wise grow never old, even though they age in the physical realm.

Seven Principles Of The Universe

1. The *all* is *mind*-mental, mentality. The Universe is all mental.

2. As above so below and vice versa.

3. Nothing rests, everything moves and vibrates.

4. Everything is dual, has polarity, pairs of opposites. All paradoxes may be reconciled.

5. Everything flows, has tides, has pendulum swing. Rhythm compensates.

6. Every cause has its effect. Every effect has its cause.

7. Gender is in everything, on all Planes, everything has its masculine and feminine principles.

Signposts for the Soul

This is a completely different use of Tarot cards, having nothing whatever to do with Divination, in the strict sense of the word. It encompasses Numerology, in addition to having emphasis placed on the actual card whether Major or Minor, as a key to knowing oneself, and to expand on this information, by meditating on the cards individually.

You have a Personality card, Soul card, and several others, as you work out this little system of *"Know Thyself"*, so here is how to do it:

To find your Personality card, add together your birthday, month and year as shown:

Born 29-3-1929:

29+3+1929 = 1961

Then add each of the digits of the total:

1+9+6+1=17

The Tarot Trump card 17 is the card called the Personality card, for this birthday.

You do this with any total from one to twenty two. If the answer is more than 22, you reduce the sum again.

For example:

Day 29. month 9. year 1938. The sum of these figures is 1976. So this gives a total of 23. This you then reduce again, by adding the two figures together, which gives a final number of 5. This is then the Personality card.

This method of adding all the numbers of a birthday together is exactly the same as that system used in Numerology.

Now we come to your Spiritual or Soul card. To find the right card for yourself, *add* the two digits of the number of your Personality card together.

So in the first example I gave, the number of the Personality card was 17, therefore the Soul card will be card number eight, 1+7=8.

In the second example I gave, the number of the Personality card was 5, and in this sort of instance, this is also your soul card number.

What this implies is that in this lifetime, you should be working on your Spiritual development, in whatever manner is suggested by your Personality/Soul card.

There is one exception to all the above:- If the number of Personality card is 19, then in *This instance only*, cards 19, 10 and 1, all apply to you, and they are *all* both your Personality and Soul cards.

An example of this is:

Day: 12
Month: 11
Year: 1931
This birthday totals: 1954
(12+11+1931 = 1954)
1+9+5+4 = 19

This card number 19 now becomes both Personality and Soul cards, and *also cards* 10 and 1.

If 19, 10, and 1, happen to be *your* cards, then a great deal of thought is required in order for you to discover and also understand the way your life should be going.

Having these cards is very significant, and can be most rewarding in a spiritual way for you. Meditating on these cards will help you to see the path before you.

If your Personality card is 22, then The Emperor is your Personality card, and the Card 0, *the fool* is your *soul* card.

When you have this combination, you really have to make a choice between the material gains epitomised by the Emperor, or the great spirituality represented by the Fool.

When you have worked out your numbers, do take some time to study the relevant cards and see what their symbology means to *you*. Then meditate on them. It is a good idea to keep a diary just for the information and insights gained during meditation.

Now you can discover your year card. This is done by taking the day and month of your birthday and adding the current year, or next year if you wish.

It is the same as for the Personality card, except you change the year of your birth, to the current one or next year. Make a note of this card also, and think about the card itself-its significance and story, but also how it relates to your Personality and Soul cards.

Are they in opposition? Are they in tune-harmonious with each other? Is one in harmony and one in opposition and if so which one is harmonious?

From this information can be deduced, to a certain extent, what kind of year and how to approach it.

There are twelve Major Arcana cards which apply to the Signs of the Zodiac. This is also part of your Metaphysical Profile so I list them here, and your Sun Sign card should then be added to the others.

Sun Sign	Trump	Card Number
Aries	Emperor	Four
Taurus	Hierophant	Five
Gemini	Lovers	Six
Cancer	Chariot	Seven
Leo	Strength	Eight
Virgo	Hermit	Nine
Libra	Justice	Eleven
Scorpio	Death	Thirteen
Sagittarius	Temperance	Fourteen
Capricorn	Devil	Fifteen
Aquarius	Star	Seventeen
Pisces	Moon	Eighteen

We now come to the Trumps Minor or Minor Arcana of the Tarot deck, but before looking at these, I will summarise what you have so far. You have your Personality and Soul cards, how to find the year card, for the current or next year, and the card that applies to your Sun Sign. All these cards are from the Major Arcana, and they can be seen as Archetypes or Archetypal influences in your life. They are part of the Unseen World, but the Minor Arcana are more concerned with your life on the Physical Plane. So the Minor cards are of a more mundane nature than the Major ones. They are more concerned with your everyday life, although the spiritual side of you is of course, there all the time.

The Minor Arcana

ARIES

March 21-30	Two of Wands
March 31-Apr.10	Three of Wands
April 11-20	Four of Wands

TAURUS

April 21-30	Five of Pentacles
May 1-10	Six of Pentacles
May 11-31	Seven of Pentacles

GEMINI

May 21-31	Eight of Swords
June 1-10	Nine of Swords
June 11-20	Ten of Swords

CANCER

June 21-Jul.1	Two of Cups
July 2-11	Three of Cups
July 12-21	Four of Cups

LEO

July 22-Aug.1	Five of Wands
August 2-11	Six of Wands
August 12-22	Seven of Wands

VIRGO

August 23-Sept.1	Eight of Pentacles
September 2-11	Nine of Pentacles
September 12-22	Ten of Pentacles

LIBRA
September 23-Oct.2 Two of Swords
October 3-12 Three of Swords
October 13-22 Four of Swords

SCORPIO
October 23-Nov.1 Five of Cups
November 2-12 Six of Cups
November 13-22 Seven of Cups

SAGITTARIUS
November 23-Dec.2 Eight of Wands
December 3-12 Nine of Wands
December 13-21 Ten of Wands

CAPRICORN
December 22-30 Two of Pentacles
December 31-Jan.9 Three of Pentacles
January 10-19 Four of Pentacles

AQUARIUS
January 20-29 Five of Swords
January 30-Feb.8 Six of Swords
February 9-18 Seven of Swords

PISCES
February 19-28 Eight of Cups
March 1-10 Nine of Cups
March 11-20 Ten of Cups

These cards are your *"Karma"* or *"Destiny"* cards, they are important and should be included in your notebook. If you have a card such as the Five of Cups for example, look at it and remind yourself that what has gone has gone, but that you have something to look forward to. You may also give some attention to the actual *number* of the card, and see how this is interpreted in Numerology.

The two other cards that apply to your sun Sign are of course important to you, but they have less input in your life than the one that applies to the actual date. These three cards together, are a little message about how your life should be evolving. In Libra for example, the Two of Swords says one must have faith in the Guardians of the Unseen World, and believe that all is for the best. I know this can be very hard, but it is so. The Three of Swords tells us that we must not put power before all else. This may only manifest in a small way if one is not in charge of a great industry for example, but it can apply to an over-bearing spouse or bossy parent.

The Four of Swords is aptly named *"Rest from Strife"*, and indicates that one's life can be much more harmonious, if the lessons of the other two cards are acted upon.

Now linked in with your Destiny card is your Soul card number. If you take this number and apply it to the Minor Arcana, you will have four more cards. One from each suit, that will give an indication of what area in life you may find opportunities, or what in your life should be improved.

So if your Soul card number is eight-Strength - in the Major Arcana, you can now look at all the eights in the Trumps Minor, to interpret how you should be dealing with your life, its problems and its triumphs.

See next page for a chart that you can fill in for yourself.

Working Out Your Tarot Cards

The day I was born:
The month I was born:
The year I was born:
Equals:

Add each digit :   (If over 22 add again)

My Personality Number is :

The card from the Trumps Major is :

If this is a double digit add again for your *soul* number

My Soul number is :

The Trumps Major card is :

My Sun Sign card is :

My Destiny/Karma card is :

My year card is :

My two other Sun Sign cards are :

and :

My Trumps Minor cards for my triumphs and problems are
the .... of Wands, Cups, Pentacles and Swords.

Some users of this system make a Mandala out of the cards, by putting them in the order of alternating the Major cards with the Minor.

The advantage of utilising the Tarot in such a way as this, is that it encompasses both Tarot and Numerology, and has more to say about the *person* than the more conventional use of the cards does. In many ways, it is more helpful than having a Reading of the cards.

Universal Fluid Condenser

I expect most readers have seen by now with this and my other books, that I generally only use natural water for consecrating and other uses for fluids. However, when making perhaps a *"magic mirror"*, most Pagans use a Fluid Condenser to wipe it with, in order to give it a boost. Therefore, I include here a Universal Fluid Condenser, that is used by several people I know including those of the Druidic Path, and does seem to have the desired effect when used.

Eyebright	Air	Sun	Clairvoyance
Cinnamon	Fire	Sun	Protection
Camomile	Water	Sun	Meditation
Sage	Earth	Jupiter	Healing
Mullein	Fire	Saturn	Protection
Meadowsweet	Water	Mercury/ Jupiter	Love
Mugwort	Air	Venus	Protection/Clairvoyance
Juniper berries	Fire	Sun	Protection
Sandalwood Oil	Air	Moon	Protection, Healing, Purification
Juniper Oil	Fire	Sun	Protection
Cedarwood Oil	Fire	Sun	Purification, Healing, Protection, Sanctifying.

I have not worked out the relevance of the herbs, although Eyebright and Mullein both belong to the same order of herbs, as do Mugwort and Camomile. This may of course have nothing to do with their esoteric use.

All herbs and berries should be simmered in rain or river water for about an hour. This should be done during the waxing, or at the full moon. Add 3 to 5 drops of each oil and stir briskly with your athame. Ideally the herbs should *not* be brewed in an aluminium pan. The strained fluid should be kept in a dark bottle with a cork. It can be used for painting the backs of magic mirrors when consecrating, or even instead of water for hag stones, talismans etc.

Personally I think this is more ceremonial magic than pure Craft, but this particular 'brew' was given to me by a druid friend so it should at least have some virtue in it!

A Blessing For Circle Closing

May the Moons silver light shine on your way,
May the Maiden cheer you, the
Mother comfort you, the Crone guide you;
May the golden Sun warm you,
The Light Lord strengthen you by day,
The Dark Lord welcome you when twilight falls.
May the dew refresh you and the stars wisdom guide you.
May your shadow never grow less.

Index

FREE DETAILED CATALOGUE

A detailed illustrated catalogue is available on request, SAE or International Postal Coupon appreciated. Titles are available direct from Capall Bann, post free in the UK (cheque or PO with order) or from good bookshops and specialist outlets. Title currently available include:

Animals, Mind Body Spirit & Folklore
Angels and Goddesses - Celtic Christianity & Paganism by Michael Howard
Arthur - The Legend Unveiled by C Johnson & E Lung
Auguries and Omens - The Magical Lore of Birds by Yvonne Aburrow
Book of the Veil The by Peter Paddon
Call of the Horned Piper by Nigel Jackson
Cats' Company by Ann Walker
Celtic Lore & Druidic Ritual by Rhiannon Ryall
Compleat Vampyre - The Vampyre Shaman: Werewolves & Witchery by Nigel Jackson
Crystal Clear - A Guide to Quartz Crystal by Jennifer Dent
Earth Dance - A Year of Pagan Rituals by Jan Brodie

Earth Magic by Margaret McArthur
Enchanted Forest - The Magical Lore of Trees by Yvonne Aburrow
Healing Homes by Jennifer Dent
Herbcraft - Shamanic & Ritual Use of Herbs by Susan Lavender & Anna Franklin
In Search of Herne the Hunter by Eric Fitch
Inner Space Workbook - Developing Counselling & Magical Skills Through the Tarot
Kecks, Keddles & Kesh by Michael Bayley
Living Tarot by Ann Walker
Magical Incenses and Perfumes by Jan Brodie
Magical Lore of Animals by Yvonne Aburrow
Magical Lore of Cats by Marion Davies

Magical Lore of Herbs by Marion Davies
Masks of Misrule - The Horned God & His Cult in Europe by Nigel Jackson
Mysteries of the Runes by Michael Howard
Oracle of Geomancy by Nigel Pennick
Patchwork of Magic by Julia Day
Pathworking - A Practical Book of Guided Meditations by Pete Jennings
Pickingill Papers - The Origins of Gardnerian Wicca by Michael Howard
Psychic Animals by Dennis Bardens
Psychic Self Defence - Real Solutions by Jan Brodie
Runic Astrology by Nigel Pennick
Sacred Grove - The Mysteries of the Forest by Yvonne Aburrow
Sacred Geometry by Nigel Pennick
Sacred Lore of Horses The by Marion Davies
Sacred Ring - Pagan Origins British Folk Festivals & Customs by Michael Howard
Secret Places of the Goddess by Philip Heselton
Talking to the Earth by Gordon Maclellan
Taming the Wolf - Full Moon Meditations by Steve Hounsome
The Goddess Year by Nigel Pennick & Helen Field
West Country Wicca by Rhiannon Ryall
Witches of Oz The by Matthew & Julia Phillips

Capall Bann is owned and run by people actively involved in many of the areas in which we publish. Our list is expanding rapidly so do contact us for details on the latest releases. We guarantee our mailing list will never be released to other companies or organisations.

Capall Bann Publishing, Freshfields, Chieveley, Berks, RG20 8TF.